Access Your Online Support Material

Supporting Children with Complex Needs is accompanied by a number of printable online materials, designed to ensure this resource best supports your professional needs

Go to https://resourcecentre.routledge.com/books/9781032293172 and click on the cover of this book

Answer the question prompt using your copy of the book to gain access to the online content.

SUPPORTING CHILDREN WITH COMPLEX NEEDS

With communication and connectivity at its heart, this book equips educators with the skills, knowledge, and confidence to effectively support children with complex needs in the classroom, creating meaningful experiences and fostering life-long positive outcomes for all.

Taking readers on a journey from theory to practice, the book unpicks research and introduces the SPICE model for identifying and understanding needs across five key learning domains: Social, Physical, Intellectual, Communication, and Emotional Development. It goes on to propose a learner-centred Connectivity Curriculum, with attention given to the key aspects of planning, implementation and impact. Celebrating teaching and the power of authentic relationships as a foundation for learning, the book provides a space for readers to reflect and recharge, as well as questions throughout to consolidate knowledge and understanding.

Providing practical ideas to foster a connected curriculum within SEND settings, or to facilitate inclusion within the mainstream school, this book is a must-read for teachers and both new and experienced SENCOs looking for ways to plan for and support children with complex needs.

Julia Lindley-Baker teaches part-time at Lincoln Bishop University (formerly Bishop Grosseteste University), where she was Programme Leader in Special Educational Needs, Disability and Inclusion from 2010 to 2025.

Laura Mills is the SEND Regional Lead for the Elliot Foundation, developing SEND practice and provision across 10 schools in East Anglia with inclusion at the heart.

nasen is a professional membership association that supports all those who work with or care for children and young people with special and additional educational needs. Members include SENCOs, school leaders, governors/trustees, teachers, teaching assistants, support workers, other educationalists, students, and families.

nasen supports its members through policy documents, peer-reviewed academic journals, its membership magazine *nasen Connect*, publications, professional development courses, regional networks, and newsletters. Its website contains more current information, such as responses to government consultations.

nasen's published documents are held in very high regard both in the UK and internationally.

For a full list of titles, see: www.routledge.com/nasen-spotlight/book-series/FULNASEN

Other titles published in association with the National Association for Special Educational Needs (nasen):

AAC and Aided Language in the Classroom: Breaking Down Barriers for Learners with Speech, Language and Communication Needs
Katy Leckenby and Meaghan Ebbage-Taylor
2025/pb: 978-1-032-53196-0

The Secret Life of SENCOs: Practical Insights on Inclusion and Specialist Provision
Adam Boddison and Maxine O'Neill
2025/pb: 978-1-032-63478-4

Championing Co-production in the Design of Inclusive Practices: Positioning Children and Young People's Voices at the Heart of Education
Clare Woolhouse and Virginia Kay
2025/pb: 978-1-032-60279-0

Inclusion: A Principled Guide for Early Careers Teachers
Nicola Crossley and Des Hewitt
2025/pb: 978-1-032-59835-2

SUPPORTING CHILDREN WITH COMPLEX NEEDS

AN EVIDENCE-INFORMED AND HOLISTIC APPROACH TO CREATE CONNECTIVITY IN THE CLASSROOM

Julia Lindley-Baker and Laura Mills

LONDON AND NEW YORK

Designed cover image: Getty Images

First published 2026
by Routledge
4 Park Square, Milton Park, Abingdon, Oxon OX14 4RN

and by Routledge
605 Third Avenue, New York, NY 10158

Routledge is an imprint of the Taylor & Francis Group, an informa business

British Library Cataloguing-in-Publication Data
A catalogue record for this book is available from the British Library

ISBN: 9781032293141 (hbk)
ISBN: 9781032293172 (pbk)
ISBN: 9781003301004 (ebk)

DOI: 10.4324/9781003301004

Typeset in Open Sans
by Newgen Publishing UK

Access the Support Material: https://resourcecentre.routledge.com/books/9781032293172

CONTENTS

ACKNOWLEDGEMENTS

What a privilege it has been to finally put our ideas together and share them with you in this book.

The book would not have been possible without the wonderful children and adults we have met along the way. Thank you for the laughter, love, and for being you.

Thanks also to the publishing team at Taylor & Francis. You epitomise the meaning of patience. Plus, a nod to James Duke for creative design work.

And finally, thanks go to all educators, parents, and carers. You do an amazing job, and we hope that this book helps you on your journey.

1

Introduction

For many children with complex needs, the onus is constantly upon them to fit into a world which is not designed for their needs. Behest with difficulties in interaction, whether these be physical, intellectual, or social, society loads upon them the responsibility to adjust and conform. Challenges increase when trying to remember cultural rules, processing multiple incoming messages, sifting through the noise to interpret communication cues, exacerbated when situational expectations are constantly changing. Alongside this are the labels and descriptions used to identify them and support provision for atypical learners. These labels are often ascribed with the assumption that there is a shared knowledge and understanding of what the label means. Terminology and definitions often have personal and contextual meanings shaped by social experiences. These contested meanings can lead to ambiguities in determining provision and practice when most definitions arise through an ableist lens, viewing atypical needs and disability or impairment as a deficit.

This introduction offers a brief insight into a number of core issues, themes, and structures which are presented in later chapters in this book. Alongside discussion and suggestions for practice, there are opportunities for reflection and rehearsal of understanding – 'Give it a go' activities with answers provided at the end of each chapter.

Changing Terminology

The language ascribed to identify atypical learners within schools and society plays a significant part in facilitating educational opportunities, and ultimately, particularly in the current climate of provision, securing funding and determining support. Changing from single categorisation pre-1900s, terms such as idiot or imbecile morphed into umbrella terms from Mentally Handicapped (most used 1912–1978) to Special Educational Needs (SEN)[1] or Special Educational Needs and Disability (SEND)[2] in the UK, encompassing a wide range of differences. Globally ascribed labels or descriptors vary and include Individuals with Disabilities (USA), People of Determination (UAE). It

DOI: 10.4324/9781003301004-1

is not uncommon to find impairment used as an accepted label or term. Debate exists around the distinction between disability and impairment, with arguments favouring disability as relating to the functional limitations faced by an individual, often due to environmental restrictions, as opposed to impairment, which defines physical or cognitive limitations.

Labelling of any kind can serve to reinforce perceptions of a child's potential, which can be enabling or disabling. Neurodiversity offers an opportunity for alternative ways to consider differences and embraces the limitless variability of humans. A comparatively new term, its adoption and use should also consider the potential for misuse across society. Neurodiversity celebrates rather than shuns the unique differences between humans and how our brain receives, processes, and stores information. It embraces and acknowledges how brain development is influenced by a range of genetic and environmental factors, which we are only just starting to understand, as discussed in later chapters. Moving beyond this, the noun neurominority is used with increasing frequency in recognition of children and adults with medically labelled conditions such as Dyslexia, Autism, and Tourette's Syndrome.

A general posit throughout this book is to remember that everyone at some point has a learning need, albeit that these may be complex, simple, context-specific, temporary, or continuous. Needs may be related to several varied factors or conditions which, once met, enable us to feel safe, stable, and healthy. The ability to fulfil our needs is intertwined with our capability and the resources available. Many children and young people require additional support to achieve this sense of fulfilment, and adapted pedagogy matched to individual needs can offer this support. This support is a right as set out in the United Nations (UN) Convention (1989)[3], and specifically relates to our discussions on:

- Article 2 (non-discrimination),
- Article 3 (best interests of the child) and
- Article 28 (right to education).

Evidence-Informed Practice

There is a growing push for teachers to use evidence-informed practice in their classrooms, and it may for some readers feel, or indeed be many years since you studied theories of learning and development. To address this, certain chapters are more research-heavy and referenced than others. Arguments to support evidence-based teaching include the need to move beyond what to why. An understanding of how children learn, for example, facilitates a more knowledgeable response to planning and assessment[4]. Whilst inclusivity can be argued as 'one shoe for every foot', different needs can be best met through different pedagogies; not every foot fits into a glass slipper. It is important to compare alternative approaches, explore and review your approach and be bold in trying new strategies. Should your curiosity be piqued, we provide links to the sources in the chapter endnotes for you to explore further. Again, we acknowledge that the field of research is ever-expanding and that we offer lip service to some areas rather than an in-depth critique.

Intentions

Our aim when collating ideas for this book was to provide suggestions for building and leading experiences which produce a 'good life',[5] which translates into positive outcomes enmeshed in caring and meaningful experiences. These experiences are enriched when there is openness, joint context-sharing, plus negotiation in exchanges and relationship building[6]. We propose throughout this book that communication is the key needed to start unravelling and understanding complex needs, the foundation for positive, respectful, and hopefully reciprocal relationships; learning is a two-way street.

Reader Reflection

What is it to teach, to be a teacher? A Japanese proverb reads, "Better than a thousand days of diligent study is one day with a great teacher" but becoming, being and sustaining the role of "great" teacher can be challenging and, on some occasions, the following quote may feel more apt, "Teaching is like a rollercoaster ride: terrifying, exhilarating, and occasionally making you want to scream" (source unknown). When talking about readiness for teaching, the best starting place is yourself. How do you prepare? How do you plan? How do you cope with the sudden drop on the rollercoaster?

Experience and collaboration inform practice, and one of the main sources of support to deal with the dips is a valued mentor, someone who understands what the role demands and engages in non-judgmental listening. Not always needing to be given answers, sometimes the opportunity to let off steam, to externalise concerns, is needed. As you consider your readiness for teaching children with complex needs, please consider how ready you are for teaching and what resources you need to have in your support toolkit.

Integral to having the right tools and resources, the missing piece of the readiness jigsaw concerns our acceptance of the children in our classroom. Teaching is not only about classroom practice and planning but also about authenticity, unconditional positive regard and valuing the children we teach.

1.1 Give it a go...

Consider the following starting points and questions in relation to valuing children and their rights in the classroom.

How do you demonstrate that you are listening to children or facilitating meaningful communication?

How can you include children's views in your practice?

Do you always treat children with respect? Does your body language, volume, and tone reinforce this?

Does the learning environment suit the diverse needs in your classroom? Too busy, too noisy, inspirational, accessible?

Do you have mirrors in your classroom so that children can see themselves, imitate, and rehearse behaviours?

Is the room too hot? Too cold? Does it suit all children, especially those who have issues with understanding interoceptive messages?

Are there quiet spaces as well as active areas?

How often do you use an outdoor space as a classroom?

Are family members welcome to share lessons?

Do children have access to different resources to facilitate communication and expression?

And how often do you start your planning humour and fun?

How do you know what children really enjoy doing?

Promoting identity – try a 'Circle of Friends' activity.

Summary

This introduction offers a glimpse into the intentions and contents of this book. A key aim integral to the different chapters is to provide accessible content to support your awareness of complex needs and to build understanding and confidence in exploring approaches which can support you in practice. The strategies suggested are drawn from our combined insights as practitioners, and we hope that they can support you in your role as carer, educator, and advocate, regardless of setting, in enabling children to fulfil their potential.

Notes

1 Warnock, H.M. (1978) *Report of the committee of enquiry into the education of handicapped children and young people*. (Cmnd. 7212).
2 Department for Education and Department of Health (2015) *Special educational needs and disability code of practice: 0 to 25 years*.
3 United Nations (1989) *Convention on the Rights of the Child*. Treaty no. 27531. United Nations Treaty Series, 1577, pp. 3–178. Available at: United Nations Treaty Collection or Convention on the Rights of the Child text | UNICEF (Accessed 20 January 2025)
4 Hattie, J. (2012) 'Visible learning for teachers: maximizing impact on learning'. Routledge.
5 Ryan, R. M., & Deci, E. L. (2001). On happiness and human potentials: A review of research on hedonic and eudaimonic well-being. *Annual Review of Psychology*, 52, 141–166
6 Granlund, M., Wilder, J. & Almqvist, L. (2013). 'Severe Multiple Disabilities', in Michael L. Wehmeyer (ed.), *The Oxford Handbook of Positive Psychology and Disability*, Oxford Library of Psychology.

2

What are Complex Needs? Definitions and Interpretations

Knowledge, understanding, and confidence in meeting complex needs are constantly developing and being shaped through encounters and experience. I recall a time when I had to meet with parents to tell them that we no longer considered our setting to be the right one for their 19-year-old son. As much as we had tried over the past 18 months, we now felt that Richard, who had been assessed as 'severely autistic', wasn't happy and that it was time to consider moving on to supported living. I prepared myself for the meeting, armed with records and review outcomes, prepared for battle, anticipating a fight. The parents arrived and greeted me warmly. As I started my speech, they interrupted me and told me that they knew it was time for Richard to move on. Instead of rebukes or anger, they thanked me. They listed all the changes that they had seen in Richard during his time at college. He would now wait his turn; he didn't interrupt, and he would be calmer when coping with changes. For them, the most significant development was that they could now go out as a family, take a bus, go to new social settings, have a drink in a pub, and enjoy a meal in a restaurant. Richard was learning how to adapt to 'our' social world.

There are times when, as practitioners, we get bogged down in the minutiae of administrative processes, missing the significant steps which children and young adults have made in their progress. Recognition and celebration of achievement are integral to enabling all to reach their potential by being mindful of the brief time we, as practitioners, have to make a difference. As such, collaboration with parents, carers, and other professionals is key to enabling longer-term impacts. A challenge in collaboration is establishing a shared understanding of needs and intentions.

DOI: 10.4324/9781003301004-2

This chapter explores how competing definitions and identification of complex needs may pose challenges or opportunities to support us in our varying practitioner roles. Identification and assessments facilitate meaningful interventions requiring knowledge, understanding and confidence in establishing the correct starting point, essential to best practice. Aligned with these skills is an acknowledgement of children's rights, and how children's understanding of self is crucial to our readiness for teaching and their readiness for learning.

What are Complex Needs?

Context of Practice: Including Children With Complex Needs

Achieving consensus on a definition of inclusion is problematic, and whilst the journey for children with SEND to have a recognised voice and choice in their preferred learning setting feels slow, many developments in adapting teaching to meet learning needs are progressing, being mindful of settings. Existing structures within our education system, including resourcing, staff expertise, time, assessment processes, and labelling, present both opportunities and challenges in meeting complex needs. Proposed solutions have been presented through evidence-informed research and legislated revisions to frameworks for practice. However, there is increasing recognition that the umbrella term 'Special Educational Needs' is too often used as a 'catch-all' term to describe the diverse challenges children and young people experience as they navigate their educational journey. Whilst the Code of Practice (2015) offered 4 categories of need which fit under this umbrella term, there is an intricate web of differences in explaining learning which practitioners can explore to fully understand individual pupil complexities.

Medical Definitions

An understanding of learning complexities can be approached in numerous ways. One starting point may be through examination of the standard classification of mental disorders set out in the Diagnostic Statistical Manual (DSM)[1], now in its fifth iteration (revised 2022), used predominantly in the USA. Alternatively, we can reference the International Classification of Diseases (ICD) 11[2] or the International Classification of Functioning, Disability and Health (ICFDH)[3]. All three documents provide extensive insights into many different aspects of human development, classifying diseases and disorders (nosology) in relation to cause (aetiology), mechanisms by which the disease is caused (pathogenesis) or by symptoms. However, if we were to 're-run the tape of history over and over again, the DSM and ICD would not likely have the same categories on every iteration'.[4]

Reliable or Questionable Explanations?

Debates continue around the validity, reliability and application of such classifications in identifying complex needs, given that definitions predominantly focus upon either clinical or medical explanations without sufficient consideration during assessments of environmental causation. More recently, the availability of education resources, including self and/or parental assessments, has been added to the DSM website (2023), where the scoring of frequency of various presenting symptoms may present a 'diagnosis'. Research[5] suggests that these assessments can be adapted for preschool children as young as two to measure symptoms, disorders and disability. However, it is still uncertain as to how these assessments fully support families and children[6] and prompt further considerations as to how relatable and helpful such assessments are in the diagnosis of needs or in aiding collaboration and offering support in classroom settings (Article 18; parental responsibilities and state assistance).

Reader Reflection

Reflect for a moment on the following broad descriptors from the two most popular classification systems used worldwide. Read the descriptions below in relation to 'mental disorder', noting the **annotated** variations.

DSM-5 (2013)	*ICD 11 (2022)*
A mental disorder is a syndrome characterized by clinically significant disturbance in an individual's cognition, emotion regulation, or behavior that reflects a dysfunction in the psychological, biological, or developmental processes underlying[7,8] mental functioning. Mental disorders are usually associated with ***significant*** distress or ***disability*** in social, occupational or other important activities (p.20).	Mental, ***behavioural and neurodevelopmental*** disorders are syndromes characterised by clinically significant disturbance in an individual's cognition, emotional regulation, or behaviour that reflects a dysfunction in the psychological, biological, or developmental processes that underlie mental and ***behavioural*** functioning. These disturbances are usually associated with distress or ***impairment*** in ***personal, family, social, educational***, occupational, or other important areas of ***functioning*** (p.388).

While there are noticeable similarities, DSM-5 directs attention to the emotional impacts and possible relationship of a mental disorder to disability. The ICD-11 clusters syndromes and directs attention to the impact of the 'disorders' upon behaviour and ability to function, emphasising capabilities alongside medical impacts. The ICD-11

(2022) does evidence marked changes and greater alignment with the DSM-5. However, with variations in medical definitions, their value in supporting and informing classroom practice may be compromised. Future research might 'elucidate the advantages and disadvantages of alternative concepts or definitions where both DSM-5 and ICD-11... are assessed against a set of benchmarks of validity and utility'.[9]

Reader Reflection

How do you identify a child's individual needs?

Could different definitions lead to different assessments, and if so, potentially mis-diagnosis of a child's needs?

Does a medical label help you to fully understand the child's needs?

Definitions in UK Legislation

An alternative, more generalised starting point for explaining complex needs can be found in legal guidance, which relates to environmental factors, having a focus upon differentiation by location rather than condition or medicalisation of need.

> "Special educational provision", for a child aged two or more or a young person, means educational or training provision that is additional to, or different from, that made generally for others of the same age....
>
> *(Section 21, Children and Families Act, 2014)*[10]

Or by reference to definitions of the umbrella terms, which have changed little from the original descriptor in the Code of Practice (1994)

- **Special educational needs (SEN):** refers to where any pupil needs special educational provision as a result of a learning difficulty or disability.

to its current iteration (2015),

- **Special Educational Needs and Disability* (SEND):** refers to where pupils have SEN, as well as to where pupils with a disability don't have SEN[11]

This distinction between SEN or *SEND would suggest differentiation in relation to identification and assessment; however, a lack of clarity pervades the Code of Practice

(2015), with ambiguity in terminology from the cover page, '**and** disability' versus '**or** disability' which continues throughout the document.

Defining Complex Needs

Adopting the term SEND here, our experiences of teaching children with SEND concur with the aspiration of joined-up practice, that provision is more effective when collaboration between support services is in place to meet complex needs and addressed through targets set in a child's Education, Health, and Care Plan (EHCP). An EHCP is a legal document that identifies support and intended outcomes available for a child or young person up to 25 (DfE, 2015). This sense of collaboration or connectivity can support classroom practice, particularly where there is a shared understanding of the nature of a child's needs. Complex needs are defined by the National Health Service (NHS)[12] as,

- Multiple (not just isolated to one domain, such as mental and physical health);
- Persistent (long-term rather than transient);
- Severe (not responding to standard interventions); and
- Framed by family and social contexts (early family disruption, loss, inequality, prevalence of Adverse Childhood Experiences).

This definition covers both within-child and external factors, which can provide a starting point for practitioners. Again, finding a consensus for a definition of complex needs can be confusing when ensuring effective collaboration between school, health and social services.

An exploration of recent UK Government reports (2023–24) sees the term complex needs used interchangeably and in association with SEN, disability, vulnerability, health, trauma, liberty[13] and challenging behaviour and/or including autism, learning disability, and associated disorders[14] However, recognition is given that 'the most complex needs may not fit into neat categories or descriptors'[15].

Reader Reflection

Could the broad and sometimes interchangeable use of the term Complex Needs impact upon development and effective implementation of EHCPs or their equivalent?

Are there benefits to having this fluidity in the definition of Complex Needs?

Changing Definitions and Terminology

Disability can be seen as a social construct created as a means of defining norms and categorising children due to differences. Intelligence was one historical determinant in identifying differences and was perceived as a 'given', an innate ability determined at birth which could be measured (see Darwin and Galton). In 1904, Spearman published a two-factor theory of intelligence, g – general and s- specific, with each factor having different sub-sets. This fixed and limited explanation of intelligence expanded to identifying multiple intelligences as opposed to one cognitive capacity[16]. The question of agreeing on what intelligence is or how to measure it, in one or more forms, remains an area of curiosity for psychology and neuroscience. Binet (1908) is accepted as having designed the first working test to measure intelligence, introduced to assess French children identified as 'abnormal, slow rather than sick'. This medical diagnosis alone would define a child as either an idiot or an imbecile, which later changed to mild/moderate or severe if their measured intelligence quotient (IQ) assessed them as deviating from the mean of 100 (almost 2/3rds of the population score between 85 and 115).

The fifth edition of the Stanford-Binet test was released in 2003, and although the original intent has been manipulated, it is still used frequently worldwide. The test measures five weighted factors to determine cognitive strengths and weaknesses:

- Fluid Reasoning;
- Knowledge;
- Quantitative reasoning;
- Visual-Spatial processing; and
- Working Memory.

Alternative assessments available include the Wechsler Preschool and Primary Scale of Intelligence (1967) or the Bayley Scales of Infant Development, which have been trialled in relation to suitability for children with SEND and suggested as of value for working with complex needs is the adapted Bayley-III-NL-Special Needs Addition (Bayley-III-NL-SNA)[17]. These scales explore cognition, language, motor, social-emotional, and adaptive behaviour development.

2.1 Give it a go...

The story has it that when completing an IQ test, one child marked all answers as correct when asked which of the following can fly? A) Elephant B) Bird C) Horse.

What is your answer to the question?

See end of chapter for answers

Beyond Just IQ

Whilst many intelligence assessments require training and expenditure for use, it is possible to see the recurrent areas of development integral to such assessments, which support development and expand from intelligence to consideration of the whole child. Many of the revised/adapted versions now consider how both environment and experience significantly alter intelligence and cognitive capability.

Dynamic Assessment (DA) is an alternative approach to consider incorporating into teaching children with complex needs. It differs from other assessments in that it evaluates learning potential alongside existing skills. It is a hands-on, interactive process based on the premise that cognitive abilities are modifiable. Drawn from the work of Vygotsky and integral in the work of Feuerstein[18], it considers interventions to improve learning rather than simply assessing what a child can or cannot do.
DA explores

- thinking,
- perception,
- learning and
- problem solving

Active teaching processes which modify cognitive functioning and enhance learning potential are proposed to work alongside the assessment of capabilities. The coherence between assessment and intervention as identified in this approach is invaluable when working with children with complex needs, particularly when aligned with the possibilities of varied abilities and multiple intelligences. As teachers, we need to identify what each child is capable of, their strengths, and find ways to enable them to achieve their full potential (Article 29: goals of education). Their possibilities are stifled by limited opportunities to explore and engage with the world around them. Our responsibilities include searching for new ways to mediate learning[19] and create possibilities rather than looking back at what has not been achieved.

Labels, Identity, and Intelligence

In the 1960s TV series, The Prisoner, a former government agent is captured and imprisoned in a beautiful yet bizarre and mysterious community. Little is known about his secret identity and he along with his captors is known only by a number. As he repeatedly tries to escape, he is traumatized by his loss of identity, he 'will not be pushed, filed, stamped, indexed, briefed, debriefed or numbered'. The conflict between individuality and authority are heard during the opening of each episode when Number 6 says: 'I am not a number; I am a free man'.

The dilemma of who we are – the paradox of identity – is central to recognising the individual nature of each child in our classroom. They are not a number, a label, or a category. Traditional learning for children with complex needs is premised on assessing a child and then transmitting knowledge based on a medical label. A child-centric approach embraces the social nature of learning and is concerned with social dialogue. Child-centred, connected learning involves shaping teaching which embraces differences and offers personal rather than universal meaning, learning is something which occurs 'with' as opposed to 'on' someone. Labelling and the language we use in the classroom establish the learning expectations. The term 'cognitive development delay' refers to the condition of children who have not reached several of the expected milestones for their age. We become attuned to hearing delay as a deficit and potentially associate the label with limitations as opposed to possibilities. Remember, this is a very subjective concept that does not take a child's unique development journey into consideration.

2.2 Give it a go...

What is the primary difference between traditional learning approaches and child-centric approaches for children with complex needs? Select your answer...

A. Traditional learning focuses on social dialogue, while child-centric learning is based on medical labels.

B. Traditional learning assesses a child based on a medical label, while child-centric learning embraces the social nature of learning and focuses on personal meaning.
C. Traditional learning involves shaping teaching to embrace differences, while child-centric learning transmits knowledge universally.
D. Traditional learning occurs 'with' someone, while child-centric learning occurs 'on' someone.

See end of chapter for answers

Identity

The classroom environment and the relationships within a school contribute to how a child identifies and understands who they are (Article 8; protection and preservation of identity). Identity formation is not a passive process, and for a child with complex needs with limited choices, their sense of who they are is dependent upon a very narrow range of social relationships, where a majority of these are likely to be interactions with professionals rather than self-selected personal friendships. The ability and opportunity to self-determine relationships and connections are limited by the socio-cultural contexts in which they live and learn (Article 15; freedom of association). This lack of control and power can, in return, reduce their satisfaction and pleasure.[20]

Erikson's influential stages of man theory sets out a linear developmental pathway in constructing identity, which is unproblematically linked to chronological age and relates to a dominant cultural archetype, e.g. white and able-bodied. Children with complex needs come in all shapes, sizes and colours. As they develop in atypical ways with spiky profiles, learning bursts, and fallow periods, as practitioners, we need to be mindful of the lens through which children perceive themselves and concern ourselves with the rich diversity offered through intersectionality rather than narrow their identity down to 'impaired or disabled'. By enabling children to understand who they are, they develop independence and autonomy (Article 12: respect for the child's views). Erikson contests that identity and role are usually established during adolescence when there is either cohesion or diffusion (confusion) and demands an integration and synthesis of the pictures and perceptions we, and children, have about our 'selves'. Commitment, as teachers, to the exploration of the known self as a learning goal for children with complex needs is required to facilitate identity formation.

Such criteria can be daunting when we consider how to enable identity formation for children with complex needs, but we can start by laying down the foundations of their awareness of space and place. Initially, children need to have a sense of who they are in relation to their physical environment.

Reader Reflection

How can practitioners balance the need to support the identity formation of children with complex needs while ensuring that their approach does not inadvertently narrow these children's identities to their disabilities?

Suggestions

Recognise the unique and diverse developmental pathways of children with complex needs.

Consider the role of socio-cultural contexts and the impact of professional relationships versus personal friendships in shaping a child's sense of self.

Discuss strategies that can be employed to foster a child's independence and autonomy, while embracing the rich diversity offered through intersectionality.

Developing Identity

Our senses enable us to receive and process information to become aware of our surroundings. This information is facilitated through our nervous system. In a considerably basic explanation, as we grow, we start to integrate incoming sensorial messages and simultaneously code them in terms of their intensity, location and duration. This integration process helps children to differentiate between pain and comfort (cutaneous sense), move around in their environment and formulate plans of action. There are two types of sensory receptors used to code messages: interoception senses within the body, and exteroception, which is our perception of external stimuli such as sound, touch, sight, etc. In forming a sense of identity, children with complex needs may require special support in being able to distinguish between the two. They need to be able to identify where their body ends and develop a sense of tension, position, and movement (proprioception) and freedom of head movement to support posture, eye movements, and equilibrium (vestibular system). Impairment in these processes not only presents as difficulties with motor movement but also in being able to differentiate between self and others and self and objects (See Chapters 6 and 7), leading to challenges in establishing personal boundaries and interaction. In addition, and of particular importance, an awareness of boundaries can help protect children and vulnerable adults from abuse (Article 19; Protection from violence, abuse, and neglect).

2.3 Give it a go...

True or False? The identity formation of children with complex needs is primarily influenced by their interactions with professionals rather than self-selected personal friendships.

See end of chapter for answers

Complex Needs and Learning Domains

As discussed earlier, identifying what is meant by complex needs is complicated. Differing historical, psychological, and philosophical arguments shape our understanding. This is then bound up in economic, political and social contexts which drive the need for categorisation and labelling. An important argument in teaching and supporting is not so much *what*, but *how.* Understanding how children develop and learn is a fundamental aspect of planning for teaching, particularly for atypical learners. Learning is a continuous developmental process requiring firm foundations. These foundations evolve pre-birth across all learning domains, intellectual, physical, emotional, and social capacities and continuously, albeit at different paces, throughout life. A connected curriculum, as discussed later in the book, identifies ways to plan for different learning domains and needs in relation to Social, Physical, Intellectual, Communication, and Emotional development (SPICE) development which are shown in Figure 2.1.

Recognising the interconnections between these 5 developmental domains is significant in understanding the *how* alongside the *what*. These interconnections are explained by considering how research into brain architecture, genetic and multi-sensory needs, supports our understanding of developmental learning processes associated with complex needs and how learning theories can support us on our teaching journey.

Defining Needs

As alluded to before, we all have unique needs at various times. The context of where these needs present themselves can either ease or exacerbate their intensity and our

motivation to address them. Too hot, we may remove a jumper, but too cold, put on a jumper. Like Goldilocks in the story of the three bears, we consistently strive to find our own balance. Needs, as opposed to wants, may be simply explained as that which is a necessity for survival or as the gap between current and preferred status. However, if we look at needs in greater depth, we can see that it is an inherently complex concept, and numerous definitions are available[21]. As practitioners, we are balancing an array of needs presented by the child, swaying between SPICE domains. Determining a priority is challenging when planning for children with complex needs, but it is essential for sequencing learning steps and goals. This process is underpinned by observations and assessments of the child, ideally in different environments and group settings. Factors which shape needs include:

- Culture
- Language
- Identity
- Health and wellbeing
- Interests and motivation
- Functionings (resources) available.

From a humanist perspective (Maslow), we need to have our basic physiological (survival) needs met before we can engage in the fulfilment of wider needs, safety, love, esteem, and self-actualisation (creative and intellectual). In contrast to more traditional visual presentations of a hierarchy of needs, we suggest as practitioners that needs are fluid and varied in a classroom, presenting in behaviours for learning or disengagement

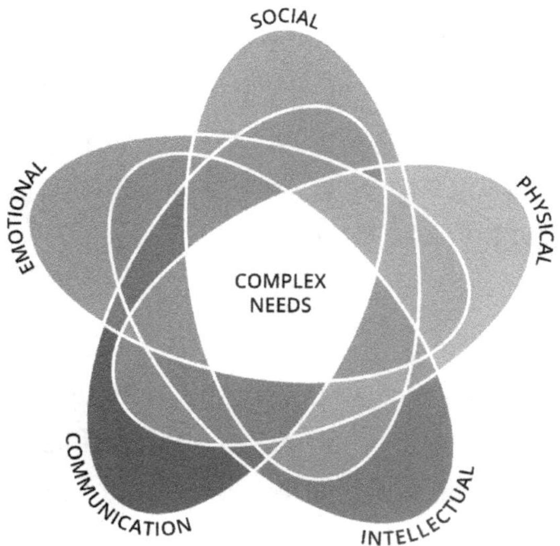

Figure 2.1 SPICE: Learning Domains

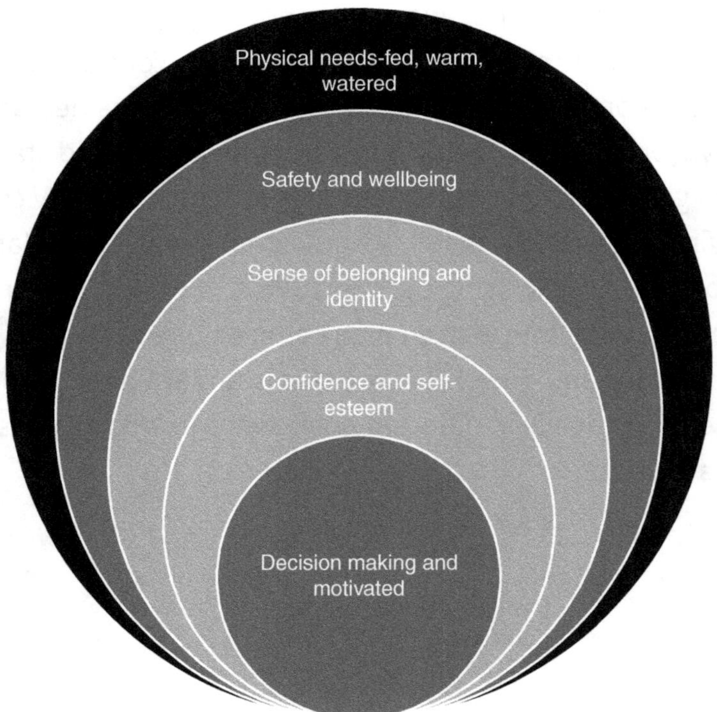

Figure 2.2: Needs and fulfilment

if not fulfilled (see Figure 2.2). The primary needs of not being hungry or thirsty need consistent reviewing throughout the day. Research posits that keeping hydrated improves cognitive functioning, although it is difficult to be accurate in determining this correlation for ethical reasons when conducting research about children[22]. However, the physiology of children, and their body surface being greater than their weight, along with the ability to store large volumes of water, suggests that children are more prone to dehydration. Dehydration may impact memory, energy and mood.

Safety and wellbeing are discussed in Chapter 5, recognising that a child needs to feel secure and free from threats to be ready to learn. Identity, as discussed above, builds confidence and self-esteem. Knowing who we are and having rewarding relationships facilitates risk-taking and coping strategies, which ultimately promote engagement in learning and intrinsic motivation and curiosity.

Unfulfilled Needs

Hangry was added to the Oxford English Dictionary in 2018. Meaning irritable or bad-tempered due to hunger, it is an example of an unfulfilled physiological need. Whether hangry, angry, or withdrawn, children present a range of behaviours which detract them from engaging in learning. Children with complex needs may have

greater difficulty in expressing their unfulfilled needs or knowing how to convey their needs in a socially acceptable way. When conditions for learning are met, children feel positive, experiencing eustress, a beneficial state with the right balance of need fulfilment supporting the gap between current and preferred status. However, when conditions change or are not present, children can present as, or become, anxious and stressed. The smallest of triggers can tip the child from optimal performance to distress (Figure 2.3).

There are numerous ways to explore the triggers or causes of stress and disengagement in learning and solutions for coping. A traditional classroom may depend on a behaviourist approach based on responding and reacting on impulse, reinforcing learned behaviours. However, it is often worth adopting a transactional approach requiring a sequence of observation, reflection, and evaluation. In essence, thinking before acting (see Figure 2.4).

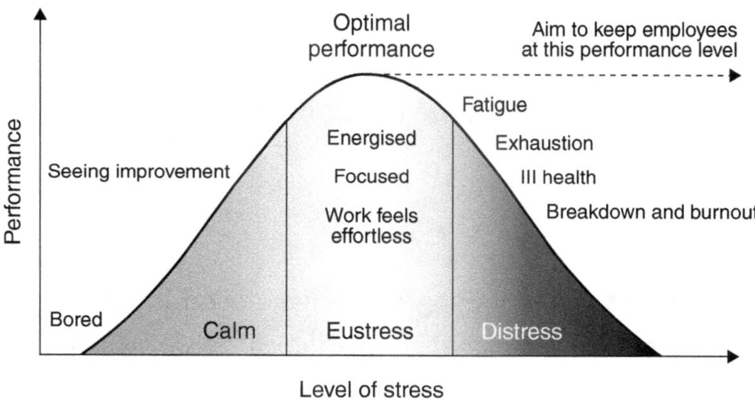

Figure 2.3 Levels of Stress and Optimal Performance

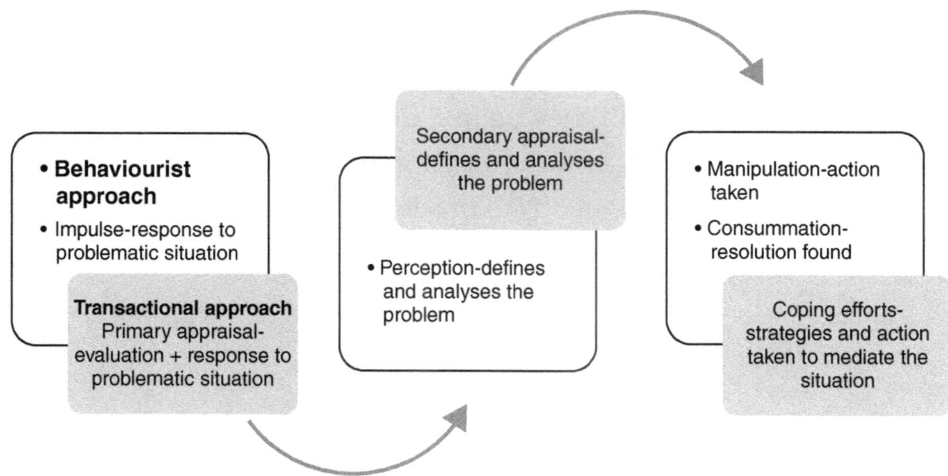

Figure 2.4 Responding to Stress

There is no glass slipper here. One approach may not fit every child or every situation. As practitioners working with complex needs, an approach that works one day may not be effective the following day. However, the starting point is building a safe environment where children feel confident to take risks and are supported in understanding who they are, building and celebrating their unique identity.

Reader Reflection

What are the various behaviours children might exhibit when their physiological needs are unmet (e.g. hunger, thirst, sleep)?

Consider children with complex needs. How might their behaviours differ, and why might they struggle more with expressing their needs?

What can you do in your classroom environment to create conditions which provide a sense of calm and safety?

Think about the small triggers that can tip a child from optimal performance to distress. List some examples and describe their potential impact.

Summary

This chapter introduced the competing challenges faced in defining complex needs. Early medical identification may lead to a medical label which supports pediatric interventions and support. Medical screening, prenatal and in the early years, can offer invaluable opportunities to foster typical childhood patterns of development. Practitioners, when working in collaboration with parents and carers, can deliver meaningful assistance at the right time. This assistance can be planned in relation to the 5 domains of SPICE to ensure needs are being met. However, not all needs present themselves in early childhood, nor can they be met during that time. As teachers or other professionals working with children with complex needs, we are striving for the optimal time to introduce adapted interventions to maximise learning potential with minimum stress.

Give it a Go: Answers

2.1 **All of them** – the given reasoning was A) Dumbo B) Bird C) Pegasus. Arguably correct, this example highlights the potential ambiguity of using IQ tests.

There are numerous online versions where you can test your own IQ or explore the (pricey) Stanford-Binet Test or select from free assessment tools if you prefer to identify a baseline for planning your interventions.

2.2 **B.** Traditional learning assesses a child based on a medical label, while child-centric learning embraces the social nature of learning and focuses on personal meaning.

2.3 **True**

Notes

1 Diagnostic Statistical Manual (DSM) website Psychiatry.org - DSM-5-TR Online Assessment Measures
2 www.who.int/standards/classifications/classification-of-diseases
3 International Classification of Functioning, Disability and Health (ICF)
4 Kendler, K. S. (2016). The nature of psychiatric disorders. *World psychiatry: official journal of the World Psychiatric Association (WPA)*, *15*(1), 5–12. https://doi.org/10.1002/wps.20292 p.5
5 Erkanli, A., Keeler, G., & Potts, E. (2006). Test-Retest Reliability of the Preschool Age Psychiatric Assessment (PAPA). *Journal of the American Academy of Child and Adolescent Psychiatry*, *45*(5), 538–549.
6 Ramos, C., Cabral, E., Figueira, P., & Santos, P. V. (2022) Psychometric Properties of the Parent-Report Version of the UCLA PTSD Reaction Index for DSM-5. *Journal of Child & Adolescent Trauma*, *15*(3), 627–637. https://doi.org/10.1007/s40653-021-00406-5
7 World Health Fact sheet, www.who.int/news-room/fact-sheets/detail/mental-disorders
8 World Health Fact sheet, www.who.int/news-room/fact-sheets/detail/mental-disorders
9 Jablensky, A. (2009). Towards ICD–11 and DSM–V: issues beyond 'harmonisation'. *British Journal of Psychiatry*, *195*(5), 379–381. doi:10.1192/bjp.bp.109.071241 p.379.
10 Children and Families Act 2014
11 Department for Education. (2015). Special educational needs and disability code of practice: 0 to 25 years. [PDF document]. Retrieved from [SEND_Code_of_Practice_January_2015.pdf (publishing.service.gov.uk) see pp 15–16)
12 National Health Services (2021) Career-and-Competence-Framework-CYP.pdf (skillsforhealth.org.uk)
13 Children's Commissioner for England (2024) *Children with complex needs who are deprived of liberty: Interviews with children to understand their experiences of being deprived of their liberty*. Available at: Children's Commissioner (Accessed: 30 January 2025).
14 Child Safeguarding Practice Review Panel - GOV.UK
15 Department for Education (2024) *SEND and alternative provision improvement plan*. Pg 84

16 Gardner, H. (1997). *Extraordinary minds: Portraits of exceptional individuals and an examination of our extraordinariness.* Basic Books.
17 Visser, L. (2014). The Bayley-III-NL Special Needs Addition: A Suitable Developmental Assessment Instrument for Young Children with Special Needs. *Journal of Cognitive Education and Psychology, 13*(3), 443–444. https://doi.org/10.1891/1945-8959.13.3.443
18 See Feuerstein PBH | Providing Learning Strategies | ADHD | Gifted Student
19 Feuerstein, R., Falik, L. H., & Feuerstein, R. S. (2015). *Changing minds and brains: the legacy of Reuven Feuerstein: higher thinking and cognition through mediated learning*. Teachers College Press, Columbia University.
20 Baumeister, R. F., & Muraven, M. (1996). Identity as adaptation to social, cultural, and historical context. *Journal of Adolescence, 19*(5), 405–416. https://doi.org/10.1006/jado.1996.0039
21 Asadi-Lari, M., Packham, C., & Gray, D. (2003). Need for redefining needs. *Health and Quality of Life Outcomes, 1*, 34. https://doi.org/10.1186/1477-7525-1-34
22 Secher. M, & Ritz. P. (2012). Hydration and cognitive performance. *Journal of Nutrition, Health and Aging, 16*(4), 325–329. https://doi.org/10.1007/s12603-012-0033-0.

3

Understanding Development and Complex Needs

'The moon is not a turtle Daddy', replied our three-year-old daughter, having misunderstood nocturnal when my partner was explaining aspects of the solar system. Like many parents and teachers, we gather a collection of communication blunders and howlers which we repeat on occasions to any willing audience, often to the chagrin of the child. However, we need to ensure that we handle a child's errors with sensitivity. Such mistakes and misunderstandings arise through trial and rehearsal of the different tools available to help us communicate. A message in one of my diaries from the same daughter read, 'I hope you don't dye'. Thankfully, most of our washing remained the correct colours, but this further example illustrates the complexity of mastering the English written language, comprised of 26 letters and 44 unique sounds (phonemes), with more than one way of spelling them. Take, for example, ghoti, which, when sounded out phonetically, reads as fish, 'gh' = f as in enough, 'o' = I as in women and 'ti' = sh as in emotion. Please do not get me started about how you say scones. Phonemes help us differentiate sounds and meaning, whilst letter shapes and combinations (graphemes) represent these sounds. Errors occur in both verbal and non-verbal communication, impacting learning and development across SPICE (see Chapter 1).

Communication is a means of sharing and receiving information,

- it can be context-specific,
- culturally diverse, and
- used in different formats, enabling us to make sense of our world.

DOI: 10.4324/9781003301004-3

From single syllable utterances, throwing a television set, or to the more constructive deployment of technology and, most latterly, AI (Artificial Intelligence), we strive to form connections enabling the expression of thoughts, feelings, and emotions.

This chapter examines both typical and atypical developmental theories of how we learn to socialise and interact by looking at how the brain develops, the place of genetics and the role of our senses, drawing attention to the challenges children face as both producers and receivers of information and how it can ultimately impact wellbeing. And in case you were wondering, yes, I have had to dodge not one but two televisions, on separate occasions, during my teaching career. One can surmise that the 'throwers' were communicating that they weren't particularly content at that point in their day.

Understanding how we learn is a complex process. An initial question centres upon what we mean by learning. Is it the acquisition of knowledge, the rehearsal and mastery of skills, or the ability to adapt and demonstrate those skills upon demand? Learning can embrace all of these, recognised as a continuous process, influenced by a range of factors including inherited attributes, genes, and environmental differences. An understanding of these different factors is considered here, starting with an exploration of how brain functions enable the learning process.

Exploring the Brain

Birdseed to Imaging

In the 1800s, early theoretical **deterministic explanations** of the brain held two central tenets;

1. Skull size = brain size = intelligence
2. Intelligence was fixed

Debate ensued, and Craniology followed, where intelligence was argued as being determined by the size and shape of the skull, progressing to Phrenology, claiming that measurement of bumps and lumps on the skull determined personality and characteristics.

As technology has advanced, so has our understanding of how the brain and nervous system function (neuroscience), offering possible explanations as to how we do or do not learn, and which brain structures may assist a specific learning function or behaviour. However, whilst research[1] continues to explore cerebral structural development in relation to head circumference and body length in neonates, be assured that we are not advocating that you start measuring shape, size of head, angle of the jawbone or weight of the brain to predict an individual's capacity to learn. Instead, it is worth exploring how neuroscience has progressed over the last four decades to establish several basic principles around brain development.

Starting with some important fundamentals concerning brain architecture, this chapter then progresses to consider how developments in neuroscience, genetics, and sensory learning enable teaching to be adapted for complex needs, with the occasional detour to consider myths about all three.

Brain Architecture

The human body is amazing, made of trillions of cells and possibly as many as 200 diverse types of cells, varying in size, structure, number and use, e.g. nerve cells, blood cells, and fat cells. Whilst having distinct functions, certain cells share similar structures, one of which is the nucleus, the place where most *Deoxyribonucleic acid (DNA)* and *Ribonucleic acid (RNA)* molecules are stored (the significance of DNA, genetics, and learning needs is explored later). Cells serve as the body's receptors and decoders of information, which they pass on to one or the other of the two main body parts, *the central nervous system (CNS)* or the *peripheral nervous system (PNS)*. The CNS receives and processes sensory information, which responds by sending out motor signals, resulting in a physical response. The brain is one component of the CNS, the other parts being the spinal cord and nerves.

Our brain alone is complex, consisting of nearly 200 billion cells, 86 billion of which are said to be *neurons*, and the remainder are *glial cells*. Neurons are the messengers, conveying information to and from our brain. Whilst comparable with other types of body cells, they are structurally and functionally unique. Foremost in their uniqueness is having *Axons*. These are projections from the neurons which serve to communicate with other cells across a small gap, a *synapse*, transposing an electrical signal into a chemical and, back again, once transmitted, via the synapse. The incoming messages or impulses are received by the cell via a short branch (dendrite) as shown in Figure 3.1.

The process of communicating between neurons, synaptic transmission, follows a series of stages which determine how the brain and the body should or could respond. There are 3 distinct kinds of neurons in the body:

- Motor - control voluntary muscle activity such as fine or gross motor movements,
- Sensory - carry information from the sense organs, and
- Interneurons - make the connection between sensory and motor neurons

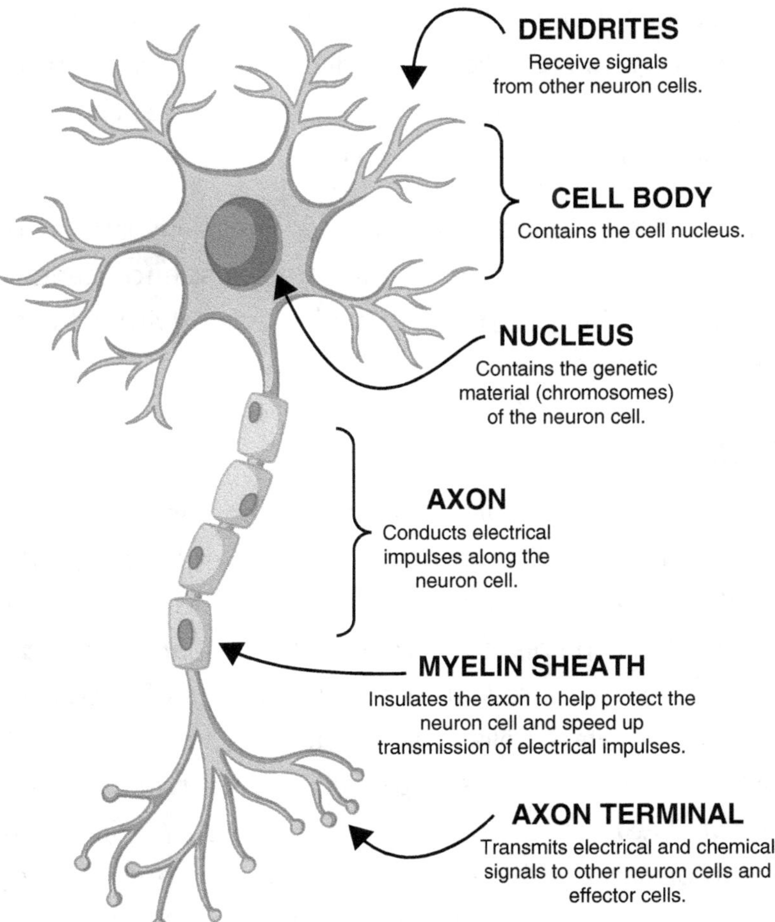

Figure 3.1 Typical neuron structure

An action potential, the neuron's response, is either stimulated, inhibited, or modulated. The ability of neurons and the brain to change, respond, rewire, and rebuild over a lifetime is defined as neuroplasticity, whereby 'cells that fire together, wire together' (see Hebb's Law, 1949).

Difficulties in the neurological processing of responses arise when the firing and wiring across the CNS are not functioning correctly. Any breakdown or interruption in the reception and response to sensory information can lead to learning complications. These complications may present in relation to one or more learning domains.

- Social (e.g. trauma-related, miscued communication)
- Physical (e.g. ataxia, poor coordination, muscle weakness [hypotonia, dystonia])
- Intellectual (e.g. epilepsy, encephalitis, Rett syndrome)
- Communication (e.g. Apraxia)
- Emotional (e.g. anxiety, somatic symptom disorder).

3.1 Give it a go

1. **What is the primary function of neurons in the human body?**
   a) To store DNA and RNA
   b) To convey information to and from the brain
   c) To act as the body's receptors and decoders of information
   d) To process sensory information and send out motor signals
2. **Which of the following statements about synaptic transmission is correct?**
   a) It involves the direct transfer of electrical signals between neurons.
   b) It converts an electrical signal into a chemical signal and back again.
   c) It only occurs in the central nervous system.
   d) It is a process unique to glial cells.
3. **What is neuroplasticity, and why is it significant?**
   a) The ability of neurons to store genetic information, significant for DNA replication.
   b) The ability of neurons and the brain to change, respond, rewire, and rebuild over a lifetime, significant for learning and adaptation.
   c) The process by which neurons communicate via synapses, significant for transmitting impulses.
   d) The classification of neurons into motor, sensory, or interneurons, significant for their specific functions.

See end of chapter for answers

Brain Development

Brain development and the formation of pathways within the CNS begin in the first few weeks after conception and continue until around the age of 30. There are critical phases of brain growth during pregnancy.

The first trimester, 1 to 12 weeks:

- The neural plate develops in the first two weeks, which grows to form the neural tube, and by Week 6, it closes to form the spinal cord.
- Millions of neurons develop electrical impulses within the brain starting around Week 8, when the baby first starts to move.
- Complications: If the neural tube does not close correctly, nerve damage and exposure to amniotic fluid can cause various developmental problems (e.g., spina bifida).

The second trimester, 13 to 26 weeks:

- The brain develops rapidly as the brain stem starts to grow, controlling breathing and the development of the lungs and other organs.
- Complications during this period may impact both the mother and baby, with the possibility of infections being transferred to the baby and leading to learning and health-related problems (e.g. toxoplasmosis and weakened immune systems and or learning delay).

The final trimester, 27 to 40 weeks (about 9 months):

- A baby's brain triples in weight and *myelin*, which increases the speed at which electrical impulses travel, and begins to coat the neurons, specifically the axons, a process known as myelination.
- Complications:
  - On rare occasions, genetic disorders such as Tay-Sachs or multiple sclerosis occur as nerve connections are impaired due to demyelination, loss of the myelin coating protecting the axon.
  - Stress, chronic illness, infections, toxin exposure, and nutritional deficiencies can result in neurodevelopmental disorders[2].

According to the World Health Organisation (WHO) (2022)[3], an estimated 1.3 billion people (16% of the world population) have a significant disability, including neurological-related needs, and in the UK, 11% of children have been classified as disabled[4]. Whilst it is difficult to identify the actual numbers, it is equally challenging to identify the precise aetiology due to developmental complexity and differences. However, we do know that the impacts of complications in brain development during pregnancy can affect a single or a combination of learning domains (SPICE).

Development in Neonates and Onwards

A newborn baby arrives with around 100 billion neurons. Neurons and messaging between the brain and nervous system are highly dependent upon the right regulation of oxygen and nutrients to function. Premature birth and/or problems during labour may result in a reduction in the oxygen supply, birth asphyxia.

Developmental complications commonly associated with a lack of oxygen (anoxia) or low oxygen concentration (hypoxia) can result in:

- Hypoxic-Ischemic Encephalopathy (HIE), which is improper brain functioning due to a lack of blood flow and oxygen at birth. It can result in a child developing a range of physical (cerebral palsy) and/or cognitive problems (epilepsy, learning delay). Extensive studies[5] report the effects of anoxia on the developing brain.
- The effects of hypoxia are less understood[6] but are related to disruptions and alterations in the development of the CNS connectivity associated with neurodiversity[7] and cognitive difficulties, including attention, learning and memory, processing speed, and executive functioning[8].

As babies acquire and rehearse skills, further myelination of neurons takes place, and the speed of conveying messages to the brain increases, and thus a skill improves. The early years are critical for activity-dependent neural development, establishing the connections between the nervous system with memory and behaviour. Whilst certain subsets of synapses are strengthened, others will be eliminated or pruned (apoptosis), a process which begins before sensory experiences develop[9].

Interactions, communication, and responsive relationships in early life experiences are significant in providing the foundations for later brain connections and well-functioning biological systems[10]. SPICE development and capacities are interwoven from the moment of conception onwards. Emotional and Social wellbeing facilitates the development of cognitive abilities, linguistic skills, and motor development. A nurturing environment strengthens the development of the brain architecture, minimising potential stressors which can impair the development of neural connections, particularly in areas of the brain which facilitate higher order skills, for example, comprehension, recall, and executive functioning.

Reader Reflection

How might difficulties in neurological processing affect a child's learning in the classroom?

Can the concept of neuroplasticity explain how learning a new skill might change the brain?

How would you use information about distinct types of neurons to understand a neurological disorder like epilepsy?

The Brain or the Mind?

What a load of 'gish gallop', a phrase coined by Eugenie Scott in 1994 to define the repeated use of inaccurate arguments without allowing any time for response. This phrase originated from debates centred around evolution and made in reference to the creationist Duane Gish when he eschewed scientific facts in favour of the religious doctrine that all living things on earth are unchanging and created by a supernatural being. This dualism between science and creationism has spurred continuous debates about the origins of man (and woman). These debates may seem unnecessary, depending upon your belief system, but they do add to the ongoing curiosity about what the brain is and how it has evolved.

In addition to this, the question of brain vs mind is a conundrum, questioned since Anaximander (610 BC) felt that the 'mind gives body a life force'. These deliberations continued until 1543, when the first anatomical drawing of the human body was produced by Andreas Vesalius. His work demonstrated that the mind and body were separate entities and not the result of vital spirits being formed in the heart and pumped into the brain (Galen, 2nd century AD). Having identified the human anatomy and the brain, developments progressed in the mid-18th century to identifying cerebral localisation, different areas serving specific functions.

Identification of localised functions evolved through the study of patients who experienced brain injury by examining before and after behaviours. Paul Broca, a French physician, having conducted a postmortem examination on 'Tan' (named because it was the only word he could say), identified damage in the left frontal lobe. Describing Tan as aphasic, the scene was set for aligning locations and functions and Broca's area became associated with articulatory language function, verbal expression. Whilst being a most frequently held explanation of how the brain works, contemporary neuroscience is questioning this, suggesting instead a network-based perspective[11]. Broca's area is now also thought to be significant in many other processing functions, including non-verbal communication, movement, and music production. In addition, research[12] identifies two processing routes in the brain for speech: auditory translations and speech comprehension.

The brain is a complex organ, and together with the spinal cord, it makes up the CNS, and it is now known that both areas are composed of;

- Grey matter – primarily made of neurons responsible for processing and interpreting information.
- White matter – predominantly axons, transmits information to other parts of the body.

Premature children may acquire a type of injury to the white matter (periventricular leukomalacia), resulting in problems with movement and other body functions. Symptoms are not always present at birth but start to show around one to two years. The most common symptom is cerebral palsy, which affects coordination and movement. Other children may have visual or learning needs. Spinal injuries also present the same symptoms, but if the neuron cell bodies are healthy, axons regrow and functions can be restored. Damage to grey matter can result in similar disabilities and is also associated with difficulties in processing information. Grey matter abnormalities may increase states of emotional and motor responses to stress[13]. A further complication to the CNS during pregnancy is spina bifida and hydrocephalus (an imbalance between the production and absorption of cerebrospinal fluid into the bloodstream). Neither of these conditions is always synonymous with complex needs, but they can create challenges related to attention span, mood swings, motor development, and fatigue[14].

Brain Damage and Atypical Learning

Our brains are constantly developing, acting as a dual carriage, conveying messages back and forth, enabling us to detect information and self-organise. Children with brain damage experience difficulties in conveying these messages and may lose some functions in movement, sensory processing and/or language. They can present with attention problems, conduct disorders and emotional swings. In addition, medical conditions such as diabetes, especially when not managed correctly, are associated with cognitive difficulties, particularly psychomotor speed, mental flexibility, and attention[15]. Table 3.1 offers a summary of how areas of the brain have been localised to serve specific functions and identifies several associated needs which may be present in the classroom.

Trickery of the Mind, Memory, and Interactions

Neuroscience is discovering a wide field of changes that occur in the brain during learning. Through advancing technology, we can now examine, in greater depth, the physiological structure of the brain, questioning localisation or networking within the brain to gain insight into how it directs a child's actions or behaviours. However, this is not yet an exact science; just as we debate what we mean by the label complex needs, so do neuroscientists contend that there is 'no neat one-to-one relationship between any one skill and any one part of the brain'[16]. As new interpretations unfold, there are still unknowns, including differentiating between the brain and the mind. The mind is said to encompass thinking, feeling, memory, and perception, distinct from the brain

Table 3.1 Brain region, functions, and damage impacts

Brain structure	*Function*	*Examples of developmental needs if damaged*
Cerebrum	Interprets sight, sound, and touch. Regulates emotions, reasoning, and learning	Wernicke syndrome (lack of vitamin B1) Hepatic encephalopathy – Reye's syndrome (liver disease)
Cerebellum	Maintains posture, balance, coordination, and fine motor skills	Motor coordination (asynergia) Judge distance and stop (dysmetria) To alternate movements quickly (adiadochokinesia) Movement (intention) tremors Weak muscles (hypotonia) Slurred speech (ataxic dysarthria) Abnormal eye movements (nystagmus)
Brainstem	Automatic functions, breathing, heartbeat	Damage to the reticular activating system leads to changes in states of consciousness, including: Locked-in syndrome Swallowing (dysphagia) Respiratory problems
Lobes/sections in the Cerebrum		
Frontal lobe	Controls voluntary movement, speech and intellect, reasoning	Personality, paying attention, organising, and switching between tasks
Parietal lobe	Processing sensory and somatosensory input (understanding the location of objects and the surroundings) and proprioception	Spatial disorientation, reading and writing problems Motor planning and spatial orientation
Temporal Lobe	Processing sensory input, including pain and auditory stimuli. Language comprehension. Interacts with and depends on messages from other brain sections.	Epilepsy, speech, and language disorders Impaired memory skills, emotional regulation and inter- and intrapersonal disorders Automatic behaviours Executive functioning Spatial navigation and reasoning.

structure. Whilst our brains enable us to do many things, they are not perfect in design. We can see this when trying to understand memory. I don't think I am the only person who has gone to a different room only to find that once there, I have forgotten what I was going for. The same happens in the classroom. We may often see a child looking back at us blankly when we ask them what they are doing. Our brain can mislead us, and our memories can be selective in what they recall, regardless of age.

Studies[17] show that whilst we confidently assert that a memory is accurate, our brains can be tricking us. This confidence comes from subconscious reliance upon various parts of our brain, to be specific, our *fusiform gyrus*, located in the temporal cortex. Being part of our visual system, it specialises in facial recognition, distinguishing between specific details of what we are looking at and enabling us to identify hundreds of different faces and respond to individual voices. Given how neurodiverse our classrooms are, it is not unusual to find that some children experience face-blindness or prosopagnosia[18]. Additionally, face-blindness may be associated with obsessive-compulsive disorders (OCD), and children might struggle to discriminate in identifying different facial expressions, particularly disgust[19].

Given that for most of us, our senses can perceive and process this information, it is amazing that we are able to connect this visual information with our language system to recall and associate names usually instantaneously. Research shows that Von Economo cells (VENs) located in the frontal cortex allow for this rapid communication between cells, particularly regarding emotional and social interactions. These cells are like our own internal emergency services, enabling the regulation of cognitive dissonance and helping with emotional judgments. These cells develop mainly after birth and continue to increase until the age of 4. Abnormal development of VENs may be attributed to social disabilities associated with neurominorities[20], children identified as autistic.

The process of remembering is very subjective, and our sense of confidence is not always a good measure of accuracy. Having delivered a 'successful learning activity', we may be frustrated when all the child recalls is the bee in the classroom, or another distraction. Children will take different aspects from an activity and not always those we had intended. This does not mean they have poor memories, but that they have processed the information differently and recall different sensations. Memory, and specifically working (short-term) memory (WM), is the retention of small amounts of information drawn through our senses and environmental cues. WM is concerned with anything which occurs in under 10 minutes. It centres upon 'living in the moment' and relies upon our *entorhinal cortex*, the part of the brain which receives and processes much of our sensory information, to do its job. The entorhinal cortex sends information to the hippocampus, presented as a pattern of firing neurons. The hippocampus jumps into action and creates a crib sheet, filtering and sorting the messages received. When these crib sheets on how to respond to the sensory information have been repeated several times, they translate into long-term memory.

So, what about being stuck in that room, trying to recall what took us there initially? As mentioned before, the brain is fallible and, on occasion, due to a variety of causes, goes into states of amnesia or forgetfulness. It is suggested that, on average, 50% of information is forgotten after one hour, 70% in 24 hours and 90% within a week[21]. To encourage retention, it is more important to consider what happens after reinforcement and rehearsal, rather than during training or learning. One reason we forget is interference, where sensory overload and too much internal noise impact both long-term recall and temporary forgetfulness. Schacter (2021) explains memory lapses as the seven sins (Table 3.2).

Table 3.2 Seven sins of memory lapses

Nature of Memory Lapse – Seven Sins	*Relates to*
1. Transcience – decreasing access to information over time	Types of forgetting or omissions
2. Absent-mindedness – inattentive or shallow processing	
3. Blocking – temporary inability to access information	
4. Misattribution – attributing information to the wrong source	Types of distortion or co-omissions
5. Suggestibility – recalling inaccurate information due to leading questions or comments	
6. Bias – where recall draws upon previous knowledge or understanding	
7. Persistence	Intrusive emotional memories, stored in the *amygdala* and difficult to forget

3.2 Give it a go...

Can you identify which sin of memory lapse is occurring in the sentences below? These are not in numerical order.

1. Mark confidently told his friends a story he thought happened to him, but it was something he had seen on his way to school.
2. After a few months, Sarah couldn't recall the details of the book she read during her summer holiday.
3. When recalling her childhood, Lisa remembered her parents as being stricter than they were, influenced by her current feelings.
4. Despite trying to forget, Tom couldn't stop thinking about an embarrassing moment from secondary school.
5. John missed his friend's birthday party because he forgot to check his calendar.
6. Emma struggled to remember a previous colleague's name, even though she could picture his face clearly.
7. After hearing a detailed account of an accident, Jane started to believe she had witnessed it, even though she wasn't there.

See end of chapter for answers

Do any of the examples resonate with your own experience?

Alongside these lapses, our WM can also become overloaded, and if we don't have the backup from a list or notes, then as soon as our attention is diverted, we forget.

Reader Reflection

1. How might the concept of face-blindness (prosopagnosia) affect a child's experience in the classroom?
2. Some children can immediately recall the smallest of details about one specific topic, e.g. bus timetables or 60s music. Classed as an obsession, how does neuroscience help explain their fascination, and how can it be accommodated as a strength in your classroom?
3. How can an understanding of working memory improve learning strategies in your classroom? See later chapters for more ideas.
4. And finally, can you please tell me what I went into that room for?

Contemporary Theories of Atypical Cognitive Development

The previous section used the terms neurodiverse, neurominority, autism, and OCD. One theoretical perspective that explores these differences and warrants mentioning to avoid confusion with the discussion of the mind is the distinctively separate 'Theory of Mind' and associated atypical development in other cognitive areas.

Theory of mind (ToM) explains the self in relation to:

- understanding or misunderstandings in communication,
- the mental states of others,
- enabling predictions of interactions and appropriate responses.

It helps us understand the complex patterns and dances involved in social interactions and how we weave our way through conversations and exchanges. Imagine social interactions as a puzzle, and ToM is suggested to be the skill that helps individuals piece it all together. In the classroom, this involves fostering open and transparent ways to communicate, providing children with both conventional and alternative ways to express wants and needs. The incorporation of augmented and assistive technology supports this (see later chapters).

Providing the physical resources alone to solve the puzzle is insufficient. Consideration needs to be given to facilitating and encouraging higher-level cognitive skills, *Executive Brain Functioning (EF)*. Being able to interact socially demands mental adaptation, requiring EF, to support both the receiver and the communicator. EF enables us to process information in a timely way and determine the right action to cope with changes[22] The development of EF varies for some individuals, and they may additionally demonstrate a preference for focusing upon the finer details, unable to put the pieces together to see the full picture, *Central Coherence Theory (CCT)*.

The following vignette may help to explain ToM, EF, and CCT. A friend recently moved to England. Having driven automatic cars for many years, being a passenger with her in a manually operated car was like a wild rodeo ride around town. As she mastered the skill of clutch and gearstick, she was then confounded by roundabouts, which they don't have in her home country; she felt that cars were coming at her from every direction. Of course, she adapted to these changes with minimal road rage from other drivers. But what if you can only drive an automatic, are overwhelmed by the speed of oncoming cars (CCT) and gesturing car drivers, unable to process their behaviour (EF), or are oblivious to it (ToM). Your default coping strategy may be to avoid or stop driving altogether. This may be how neurodiverse children cope. When challenges in processing information are overwhelming, the default is to shut down. Chapter 5 explores this further and highlights several challenges children with complex needs encounter, and suggests ways to navigate these areas in planning for complex needs.

Reader Reflection

1. How does Theory of Mind (ToM) explain how neurodivergent children may navigate social interactions?
2. What are the roles of Executive Brain Functioning (EF) and Central Coherence Theory (CCT) in social interactions, and how might their development vary among children with complex needs?
3. Using the vignette provided, can the challenges faced by the friend learning to drive a manual car relate to your experiences of how autistic children process information and respond to social interactions?

Genetics, Epigenetics, and DNA

The history of our journey to understanding the significant role that genetics plays in explaining complex needs is multifaceted and contentious. Individual reputations have been lost and won in scientific battles to discover the theory of evolution and genetics, the science of genes, variations, and inheritance. Again, dating back to the ancient Greeks, speculation as to how traits were passed from parents to child was posited by Hippocrates, speculating that the body produces seeds from various parts of the body that are transmitted at conception and by Aristotle, that organisms gradually evolve to more sophisticated forms. This investigation was then notably recorded in the work of Mendel (mid- to late-18th century), an Austrian monk, botanist, and teacher. Although his original records were burned and destroyed due to political opposition and entanglements with the government over taxes, the legacy of his discovery, Mendelian Laws of Inheritance, remains. He established, through his work with pea plants (albeit using a different type of seed than Hippocrates' ideas), the principles of heredity, discovering chromosomes and that they contained recessive and dominant traits, with each trait being independent.

This quest to uncover more about genetic inheritance continued, investigating how the cells in the human body reproduce, trying to establish the specific structure of cells. In 1956, Tijo and Levan discovered that each cell in the human body contains 23 pairs of chromosomes, refuting the 48 previously claimed. Multiply that by the suggestion that the average male has 36 trillion cells[22], then we are talking A LOT of chromosomes, and it is a wonder that so few of these end up being 'wonky'. Research around the composition and structure of chromosomes yoyoed back and forth between scientists globally and most noticeably during the 1940s and 1950s, between the work of Watson, Crick, and Wilkins, and Franklin in the UK and that of Chargaff and Pauling in the USA. The chase to discover the structure of chromosomes was very competitive, and although the Nobel prize was awarded to Watson, Crick, and Wilkins for their discovery of the molecular structure of DNA (Deoxyribonucleic acid), the contributions to the race of these other notable chemists should not be overlooked.

Key Facts

- A gene is a stretch of DNA, a twisted ladder of two linked strands.
- Every cell in our body contains the same DNA blueprint of information, and its individual pattern makes each human unique.
- The pattern is created by the sequence of four nucleotide bases, which are adenine (A), guanine (G), cytosine (C), and thymine (T).
- DNA makes RNA (Ribonucleic acid) and
- RNA makes proteins (chains of amino acids), which are essential for our body, including the CNS, to function (Figure 3.2).

- Twenty amino acids, nine of which are essential, make up the proteins stored in the neurons in each cell in the human body. For example, tryptophan, tyrosine, histidine, and arginine are amino acids used by the brain to receive and transmit different neural signalling.
- The integration of action potentials, electrical impulses sent by the nerves to the brain, synaptic signals, and neurons talking to each other enables us to sense, process, and act within our environment.

The 1960s and 1970s saw the deciphering of the genetic code and the advent of genetic engineering, allowing scientists to manipulate genes in new ways. Sanger's work (1977) discovered the sequencing of DNA, which enables us to understand how it both replicates and is affected by viruses, for example, COVID-19. In 1990, The Human Genome Project, an international scientific research project, was launched with the goal of mapping and sequencing the human genome. Having a projected cost of $3 billion, the project concluded in 2003, having made tremendous progress, costing considerably more, and still leaving many questions yet to be answered.

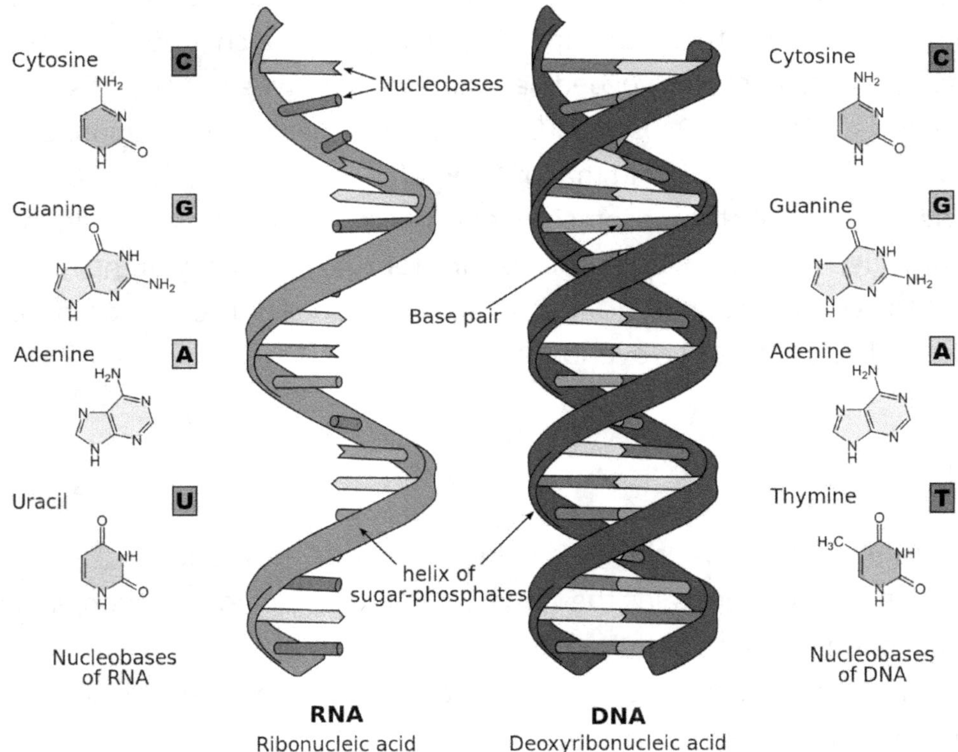

Figure 3.2 Structure of DNA vs RNA. Illustration by Roland1952, Creative Commons license CC BY-SA 3.0

3.3 Give it a go...

True or False: Hippocrates speculated that traits were passed from parents to children through seeds produced by various parts of the body.

True or False: Mendel's original records were preserved and are still available today.

True or False: In 1956, Tijo and Levan discovered that each cell in the human body contains 23 pairs of chromosomes.

True or False: The Nobel Prize for the discovery of the molecular structure of DNA was awarded to Watson, Crick, and Wilkins.

See end of chapter for answers

What We Know About Genetics and Complex Needs to Date

Genetics play a significant role in many disabilities, particularly those related to intellectual and developmental conditions. Certain disabilities are caused by *mutations* in specific single (Mendelian or monogenetic) or multiple genes (complex or polygenic inheritance). There are thousands of different mutations of single genes and plenty of room for errors. Mutations occur during cell division, and just like when we try doing different sums, cells can miss, add or replace digits in the copying process. Without the correct digits and sequencing, the sum is wrong, and the cell does not function correctly. The wrong sums can have little or significant impacts on the development of SPICE domains. We may also carry non-presenting mutations, which are not harmful as they do not change the DNA sequencing. You are probably already familiar with some genetic conditions: Down syndrome, caused by an extra copy of chromosome 21, and Fragile X syndrome, due to a mutation on the X chromosome.

Some disabilities, such as cystic fibrosis and sickle cell anaemia, are *inherited* from parents and have also been known to skip generations. Turner syndrome, where females are missing part or all of one X chromosome, presents as *chromosomal abnormalities.* Changes in the number or structure of chromosomes can lead to disabilities. Other syndromes include Klinefelter syndrome and Cri du chat ("cry of the cat") syndrome. There is a continuous debate regarding *complex genetic interactions* between multiple genes and environmental factors, which may explain a range of complex needs.

In addition, whilst the majority of DNA encodes our proteins, which tells the body what to do, recent research has identified how the previously labelled 'junk' DNA, that which does not code, still plays a functional role, and may also be a contributor to disabilities. Further research identifies that RNA, the message carrier in cells, may also be significant in atypical development. Genetic mutations can occur either randomly or due to some environmental exposure. The environmental influence on genetics is currently one of the rapidly evolving areas of research (epigenetics).

Research has identified how the human body, including our cells, has adapted, usually over many 100s of years, to environmental changes. One genetic environmental adaptation seen on a global level is the variation between communities in relation to lactose tolerance. Research suggests that different tolerances can be traced back to exposure or lack of exposure to dairy farming and products, dating back many thousands of years. At birth, most babies can digest milk without any negative reactions. The enzyme in our bodies, lactase, historically and for some populations and individuals, turns off once adulthood is reached. For communities where dairy farming and products are standard life products, the enzyme stays on, enabling the digestion of lactase without complications.

Genes are responsive to the environment, and adaptations evolve. Further genetic variations, which might be attributable to environmental changes, include music skills and artistic creativity[23]. New findings from research offer interesting consideration as to how genes influence skills and aptitude, suggesting explanations of multiple intelligences and why children, even with the most complex needs, can present abilities in different domains. Genetic disorders can vary widely in how they present in the classroom. A medical explanation of atypical development enables us to identify the cause, but it is not a teaching prescription used to define and deny opportunities. A label does not offer one fix for all.

Reader Reflection

Knowledge of genetics can help you understand the biological factors that may influence a child's learning and behaviour. This is particularly important for children with complex needs, as some conditions may have genetic components that affect their educational experience. It can support you in planning and adapting learning. Understanding these genetic connections may help in diagnosing, managing, and meeting the increasingly different and more complex needs of children in our classrooms.

What classroom adaptations may support children with the following genetic conditions?

Cystic Fibrosis: Affects the respiratory and digestive systems
Down Syndrome: **possibly** leading to developmental and cognitive delays.
Duchenne Muscular Dystrophy: A severe type of muscular dystrophy.
Haemophilia: A disorder that impairs the blood's ability to clot.

Senses

Awareness and understanding of the senses have developed from the ideas of the early Greek philosophers to the fascinating insights discovered through advances in technology and neuroscience. Aristotle (384–322 BC) originally claimed that only 4 senses mattered, and these aligned with the four fundamental elements and four qualities of which matter is composed.

- Earth – Touch and taste
- Water – Sight due to the watery nature of the eye
- Fire – Smell
- Air – Sound

This influential claim is a useful starting point for considering how children use their senses to learn and grow through interaction with their environment and is incorporated into specific philosophies and school types. Montessori, Steiner, and Forest schools promote independent and self-directed learning, holistic approaches, and connecting learning to nature and outdoor experiences. Forest schools promote immersive learning in nature to foster a deep relationship with the natural world. Integrating these approaches into teaching children with complex needs can facilitate sensory awareness and cognitive skills.

Humans have an innate tendency to seek connections with nature (Biophilia) in the same way they seek connections with other people. Research[24] shows that environmental education promotes cognitive development, emotional growth, and social integration. Children identified as autistic benefit in emotional restoration, calmness, and alertness[25,26].

Reader Reflections

To what extent do you integrate the outdoor world and the inside world in your working environment/ classroom?

Do you have children in your classes who prefer to get their hands messy, engage with repeated sniffing and/or licking objects, and even people? If so, why do they do it? Can you offer learning experiences which include but moderate certain behaviours?

A commonly held assertion is that humans have five **primary** senses: touch, sight, hearing, smell, and taste. Each sense helps us perceive and interact with the world in unique ways.

1. **Touch**: This sense is communicated through specialised neurons in the skin. It includes sensations like pressure, temperature, pain, and vibration. Touch is essential for children to explore their environment, and is now recognised as significant in supporting attachment and emotional development[27].
2. **Sight**: Sight, or vision, involves the eyes detecting light and converting it into electrical signals sent to the brain. The brain processes these signals to create images, which support children in how they perceive and navigate their environments. It facilitates non-verbal communication and interaction. It can also play tricks on us and can often override the messages received from the brain from other senses[28].
3. **Hearing**: Hearing involves the detection of sound waves by the ears. These waves are converted into electrical signals that the brain interprets as different sounds. Of course, we know that hearing facilitates communication, but it is also a complex process which enables children to identify and respond to objects in their environment.
4. **Smell**: The sense of smell, or olfaction, detects airborne chemicals. These chemicals bind to receptors in the nose, sending signals to the brain that are interpreted as different odours. Smell is intricately linked to taste and can trigger memories, emotions and alter our affective state. It is significant in detecting danger (fires, etc.). Children can be particularly sensitive to strong odours or scents. Conversely, while smell loss is quite unusual in children, it can have an impact on perceptual and cognitive development[29].
5. **Taste**: Taste, or gustation, involves detecting chemicals in items we put in our mouths through taste buds on the tongue. There are five basic tastes: sweet, salty,

sour, bitter, and umami. Taste is often a learned response, and we culturally develop to eat particular foods or avoid others. Pica is a disorder where children start experiencing the world through their mouth, eating things we don't usually consider to be food. One explanation is an iron, zinc, or calcium deficiency.

In addition to these five primary senses, humans also have other senses, including:

- Balance (vestibular sense)
- Spatial awareness (proprioception), which helps us navigate and maintain our posture
- Internal awareness of our physical state, i.e. hunger, pain (interoception).

Our senses do not operate independently; that is a myth. Instead, our brain processes sensory information through different types of receptors, following several steps involving different neural pathways.

This intricate process allows us to perceive and interact with the world around us. If the sensory pathways are damaged, then children can struggle to progress and process information at any of these stages. In addition, they will be learning how to manage physical conditions, which may include

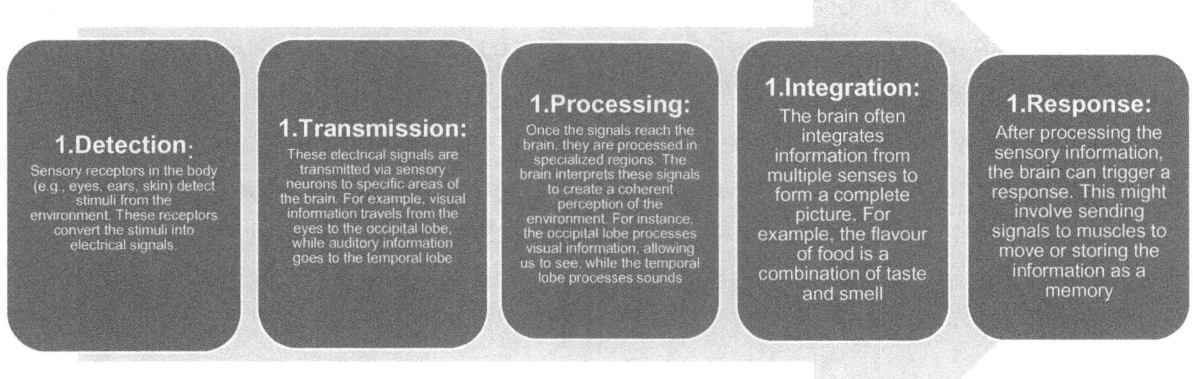

Figure 3.3 Sensory Integration

- numbness or tingling,
- loss of sensations impacting upon touch,
- temperature and detecting pain or injury (Channelopathy-associated congenital insensitivity).

Children may experience chronic pain effecting motor movements and balance and coordination problems, such as Developmental Coordination Disorder, Stereotypic movement disorder, Tourette's disorder. Motor movement problems do not necessarily result in cognitive learning difficulties.

Reader Reflection

1. Consider one activity that can help enhance a child's sense of touch in the classroom.
2. Explain why sensory development is important for a child's overall growth and learning.
3. List three sensory activities that can be incorporated into a classroom setting.
4. How can you create a sensory-friendly classroom environment for children with sensory processing issues?

Summary

Sensory development is significant in facilitating learning. It enables interaction with our environment and is influenced by both our genetic history and environment. Different areas of the brain are specialised in interpreting messages relayed from our senses. Each unique genetic makeup and chromosomal variations influence how well a child develops in all aspects of SPICE. Early identification and continued interventions which promote neural development and reconnections (brain plasticity) are essential for children with complex needs. An understanding of this interconnection and the provision of a nurturing classroom enriched with a curriculum which includes a sensory diet (see Chapters 6 and 7) will foster children's potential to learn.

Give it a go – The Answers

3.1 Functions

1. What is the primary function of neurons in the human body?
   Answer: b) To convey information to and from the brain
2. Which of the following statements about synaptic transmission is correct?
   Answer: b) It converts an electrical signal into a chemical signal and back again.
3. What is neuroplasticity, and why is it significant?

   Answer: b) The ability of neurons and the brain to change, respond, rewire, and rebuild over a lifetime, significant for learning and adaptation.

3.2 Can you identify which sin of memory lapse is occurring in the sentences below

1. **Misattribution:** Mark confidently told his friends a story he thought happened to him, but it was something he had seen on his way to school.
2. **Transience:** After a few months, Sarah couldn't recall the details of the book she read during her summer holiday.
3. **Bias:** When recalling her childhood, Lisa remembered her parents as being stricter than they were, influenced by her current feelings.
4. **Persistence:** Despite trying to forget, Tom couldn't stop thinking about an embarrassing moment from secondary school.
5. **Absent-mindedness:** John missed his friend's birthday party because he forgot to check his calendar.
6. **Blocking:** Emma struggled to remember her old colleague's name, even though she could picture his face clearly.
7. **Suggestibility:** After hearing a detailed account of an accident, Jane started to believe she had witnessed it, even though she wasn't there.

3.3 True or False

1. **True**: Hippocrates speculated that traits were passed from parents to children through seeds produced by various parts of the body.
2. **False:** Mendel's original records were preserved and are still available today.

3. **True**: In 1956, Tijo and Levan discovered that each cell in the human body contains 23 pairs of chromosomes.
4. **True:** The Nobel Prize for the discovery of the molecular structure of DNA was awarded to Watson, Crick, and Wilkins.

Notes

1 Courchesne, et al., 2004, Holland et al., 2014, Millichap & Millichap, 2014.

2 D Doi, M., Usui, N., & Shimada, S. (2022). Prenatal Environment and Neurodevelopmental Disorders. *Frontiers in Endocrinology, 13*, 860110. https://doi.org/10.3389/fendo.2022.860110

3 World Health organisation (2022) Disability (who.int)

4 Kirk-Wade, E., Stiebahl, S., & Wong, H. (2024, October 2). *UK disability statistics: Prevalence and life experiences*. Commons Library Research Briefing. https://commonslibrary.parliament.uk

5 (du Plessis, A. J., & Volpe, J. J., 2002, Back, 2014)

6 Bonkowsky, J. L., & Son, J. H. (2018). Hypoxia and connectivity in the developing vertebrate nervous system. *Disease Models & Mechanisms, 11*(12), dmm037127. https://doi.org/10.1242/dmm.037127

7 Wang, X., Cui, L. & Ji, X. (1922). Cognitive impairment caused by hypoxia: from clinical evidences to molecular mechanisms. *Metab Brain Dis* **37**, 51–66 https://doi.org/10.1007/s11011-021-00796-3

8 (Geschwind & Levitt, 2007)

9 Shatz C. J. (2009). MHC class I: an unexpected role in neuronal plasticity. *Neuron, 64*(1), 40–45. https://doi.org/10.1016/j.neuron.2009.09.044

10 National Scientific Council on the Developing Child (2020). *Connecting the Brain to the Rest of the Body: Early Childhood Development and Lifelong Health Are Deeply Intertwined Working Paper No. 15*. Retrieved from www.developingchild.harvard.edu.

11 Friedrich et al., 2019.

12 Hickok, G., Poeppel, D. (2007).The cortical organization of speech processing. *Nature Reviews Neuroscience, 8*, 393–402. https://doi.org/10.1038/nrn2113
Hickok, G., & Poeppel, D. (2015). Neural basis of speech perception. *Handbook of Clinical Neurology, 129*, 149–160. https://doi.org/10.1016/B978-0-444-62630-1.00008-1

13 Kozlowska et al., 2017

14 (Juranek et al., 2010)

15 (Moheet et al., 2015)

16 (Rippon, 2019. Pg. 29)

17 (Mendez & Fras, 2011)

18 (Stantić, 2022)

19 (Corcoran et al., 2008)

20 Allman et al (2005)

21 Kohn (2017) Brain Science: Overcoming the Forgetting Curve see Dr. Art Kohn Explains How to Achieve the Optimal Learning Experience with Boosts and Bursts - NASBA Registry

22 Hatton, I. A., Galbraith, E. D., Merleau, N. S. C., Miettinen, T. P., Smith, B. M., & Shander, J. A. (2023). The human cell count and size distribution. *Proceedings of the National Academy*

of Sciences of the United States of America, *120*(39), e2303077120. https://doi.org/10.1073/pnas.2303077120

23 Theusch, E., Basu, A., & Gitschier, J. (2009). Genome-wide study of families with absolute pitch reveals linkage to 8q24.21 and locus heterogeneity. *American Journal of Human Genetics*, *85*(1), 112–119. https://doi.org/10.1016/j.ajhg.2009.06.010

24 Stavrianos, A. (2016). 'Green inclusion: Biophilia as a necessity', *British Journal of Special Education*, *43*(4), 416–429. doi:10.1111/1467-8578.12155.

25 Hartig, T., Korpela, K., Evans, G. W., & Gärling, T. (1997). A measure of restorative quality in environments. *Scandinavian Housing and Planning Research*, *14*(4), 175–194. https://doi.org/10.1080/02815739708730435

26 Weber, S.T. & Heuberger, E. (2008). The Impact of Natural Odors on Affective States in Humans, *Chemical Senses*, *33*(5), 441–447, https://doi.org/10.1093/chemse/bjn011

27 Duhn, L. (2010). The importance of touch in the development of attachment. *Advances in Neonatal Care*, *10*(6), 294–300. https://doi.org/10.1097/ANC.0b013e3181fd2263

28 Tsay, C. (2013). Sight over sound in the judgment of music performance, *Proc. Natl. Acad. Sci. U.S.A.* *110*(36) 14580–14585, https://doi.org/10.1073/pnas.1221454110 (2013).

29 Cameron E. L. (2018). Olfactory perception in children. *World Journal of Otorhinolaryngology - Head and Neck Surgery*, *4*(1), 57–66. https://doi.org/10.1016/j.wjorl.2018.02.002

4

Explaining Learning and Missed Opportunities

Many eons ago when red roadside telephone boxes housed phones instead of second-hand books, when we ate fish and chips from newspapers and teachers had no inclination that a National Curriculum was on the horizon or that HMI visits would be supplanted by Ofsted, it was not unusual for a sunshine filled day to mean everyone in a special school classroom would pile into a minibus and head to the coast for an ice cream or candy floss. Flip-flops and kagoules would be stuffed into carrier bags as we immersed our pupils into the 'real world'. Often being met with sideways glances from strangers, pupils would jig and dance (or occasionally lie down and refuse to move), along the pavement, flapping their arms as they unsuccessfully tried to chase down seagulls. Planned lessons would be changed, and teaching would be adapted to the weather, mood, or the family of frogs arriving in a trouser pocket. Pupils would be segregated from their community to attend one or other school designated for the mentally handicapped, moderate, severe or physically handicapped, determined by medical and or intelligence assessments. In melancholy moments, it is possible to reflect upon the freedom and choices available to teachers in those halcyon school days of the last century, pining for what is lost. When looking at special and increasingly mainstream schools, 'It wasn't like that in my day', is an oft-repeated evaluation of both current practice and provision and most markedly changes in pupil characteristics and demographics on school registers.

Hallelujah!

Thank goodness times have changed. Who needs roadside phones when we have mobile ones? Fish and chips can be eaten from any receptacle. Individualised learning needs can be met through targeted interventions which incorporate sand and water play or create a sensory garden where the life cycles of amphibians are explored. Additionally, and significantly, these interventions can be informed by the

DOI: 10.4324/9781003301004-4

child or young person themselves. As a student, Denni once explained his world to me, 'Interaction for me is like crossing a bridge between two worlds. I feel like I always must cross over that bridge. What would be great is if I can meet people in the middle'.

We have progressed so much in our explorations of teaching and how we, as learning facilitators, not only immerse pupils in the 'real world' but also equip them with the skills to deal with and learn from new experiences, safeguarding them from strangers. This chapter sets out to explore theoretical explanations of what is understood about learning and how we can draw upon this in supporting children, in different settings, with diverse, complex needs, to grow.

Learning Domains SPICE

Understanding how children learn is a fundamental aspect of planning for teaching, particularly for children identified as having complex needs (Chapter 2). Learning is a continuous developmental process requiring firm foundations. These foundations evolve from social, physical, intellectual, communicative, and emotional and social capacities pre-birth and throughout life. A 'connected' curriculum (see Chapter 6 onwards) identifies learning domains and needs in relation to Social, Physical, Intellectual, Communication, and Emotional development (SPICE) (Figure 4.1).

Recognising the interconnections between these five development domains is significant in understanding complex learning needs. These interconnections can be

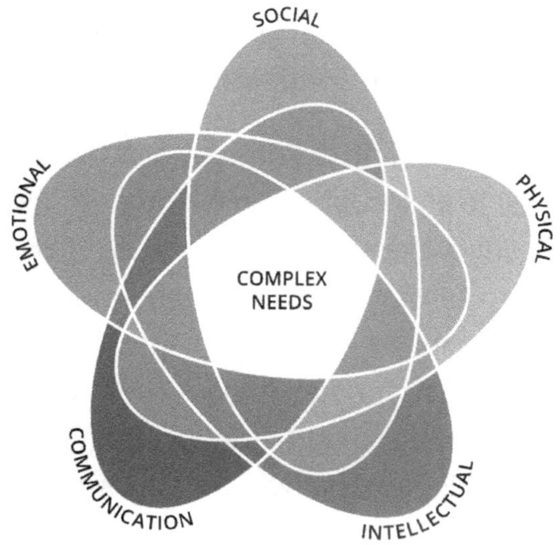

Figure 4.1 SPICE: Learning Domains

explained by considering how research into brain architecture, genetics, and multi-sensory needs (Chapters 2 and 3) supports understanding of the developmental learning processes associated with complex needs, and learning theories can support us further in a teaching journey. A key factor is to consider ways in which theories can facilitate learning, which includes all children avoiding marginalisation through overly differentiating the curriculum, and potentially segregating children due to differences[1].

This chapter explores competing and complementary theories of how children learn to learn to develop. In addition, by tracing theories of child development, it is possible to discern how explanations of typical development patterns contributed to patterns of segregation and subsequently, atypical development theories emerged.

Who Said What About Learning?

Divisions or categorisation within society and education are not a recent phenomenon, and classification of individuals due to differences in mental abilities dates to 1152 BC, when the earliest record of the term 'retardation' is found in the Therapeutic Papyrus of Thebes. As the Greeks philosophised about ways to seek a 'good or ethical life' (Socrates 470–399 BC), societal structures marked physical and racial differences as inferior. Hippocrates (460–357 BC), the 'father of medicine', first questioned whether causes of disabilities were, in fact, due to divine intervention or related to natural causes. 'Persons who have a painful affection in any part of the body and are in a great measure sensible of the pain, are disordered in intellect'[2].

Aristotle (34–322) progressed this line of enquiry studying the human form and 'deformities', which, upon scrutiny of his work, does not mean a thing of ugliness but rather a feat of wonder and marvel[3]. Galen's (130–200 AD) work was significant in understanding learning and the natural causes of disability, identifying how the brain was central to the nervous system and the development of intelligence.

As the centuries passed, understanding of anatomy and increasing scientific explanations evolved alongside philosophical explanations. The relationship between head and heart was significant in the writings of Hobbes (1588–1679), who proposed how both were interrelated to sensory responses, emotions, and intelligence. The heart was, for two millennia, considered to be the seat of intelligence[4]; its significance in managing emotions and working as innate intuitive intelligence has taken somewhat of a back seat compared to other research into how we learn and function. 'The heart is ... a source of wisdom and intelligence that we can call upon to live our lives with more balance, greater creativity, and enhanced intuitive capacities'[5].

The eventual shift from the heart to the brain as the seat of intelligence marked a turning point in scientific understanding. However, the significance of the heart as a place of intelligence is undergoing something of a renaissance and is no longer confined to romance or history. Scientific research, neurocardiology, the link between heart and brain, explores the heart's intricate complexity, revealing a sophisticated neural network referred to as the heart's 'little brain'. The communication between the heart and brain is far more complex than a simple call-and-response system. It is a constant, bidirectional dialogue that influences our thoughts, emotions, and physical state, building coherence between thoughts, emotional states, and responses[6].

Reader Reflection

Explorations of the connection between, brain, heart and our nervous systems have been fundamental in explanations of learning.

As teachers, we often use 'think' and 'feel' within the classroom, which shapes our approach to education. When we encourage students to think, we foster their cognitive abilities, critical thinking, and problem-solving skills. However, equally important is nurturing their ability to feel, which involves understanding emotions, empathy, and social interactions. By integrating both thinking and feeling into our teaching, we create a balanced learning environment that supports intellectual growth and emotional well-being. Do you incorporate both thinking and feeling into your teaching methods to facilitate coherence? Is the heart as significant as the brain in learning?

What is Learning?

Learning is the processing of sensory information to acquire new or different ways to respond to the world around us. Through interactions with our environment, we develop knowledge and skills which shape our behaviours and inform our values, attitudes, and preferences. Children are exposed to many different environments, some positive and some toxic, but all are influential in how they perceive themselves and respond. Theoretical explanations offer choices in how to create positive and meaningful experiences for children to explore and engage in their world. The following section explores theoretical explanations of SPICE, many of which are drawn from psychology.

The Origins and Influence of Psychology Upon Learning

In exploring how children learn, the nature vs. nurture debate upon which psychology was originally premised dates to the proposals of Plato (nature) and Aristotle (nurture). The idea of either/or was established further through the concept of dualism (Descartes 1956–1650), asserting that the mind and body were separate entities which become intertwined with the debate centring upon the relationship between the two. Acknowledging the contribution of the Greek sophists and philosophers, one of the earliest noted founders of current psychological theory is attributed to Charles Darwin (1809–1882), an English naturalist. Whilst not only celebrated for his theory of evolution by natural selection, he is also known to have explored how people understand the emotions of others and delved into experimental psychology, having a tremendous impact upon current thinking, particularly in relation to autism, schizophrenia[7] learning.

This dichotomy between innate and acquired functionings is present in several current psychological theories and may influence the variations in how we identify and assess a child's learning needs. Depending on the source, there are different claims as to the number of areas of psychology recognised today, varying from four, five, six, seven or as high as twenty-four[8]. This chapter explores two of the five major areas of psychology that haven't been explored elsewhere in this book, which have, and currently contribute to, a changing understanding of learning and complex needs.

1. **behavioural psychology** (understanding behaviour through different types of conditioning),
2. **cognitive/constructivist/developmental psychology** (the study of the mental processes and the environment),
3. **psychodynamic** (the interpretation of mental and emotional processes) (Chapter 5),
4. **humanistic** (exploration and understanding of self in relation to one's environment) (Chapter 2)
5. **biopsychology** (research on the brain, behaviour, and evolution) (Chapter 3).

An important assertion to accompany the explanations which follow is that not all theories are relevant to every need; in fact, we refer to them as a starting point for reflection rather than doctrines for practice.

Behaviourism

One of the founding explanations of learning, dating back to Aristotle (384–322 BCE), relates to changes in behaviour which directly correlate with an instinct or motivation to increase pleasure and avoid pain. Conditioning or modifying a response to a neural stimulus facilitates this instinct and is fundamental to the learning process.

Classical conditioning (Pavlov, 1849–1936) recognises a distinction between an unconditioned vs a conditioned response, identifying how some behaviours or reflexes are automatic, e.g. blinking, whilst others can be manipulated, e.g. learning to ride a bike or hold a pen.

Behaviourism (Watson, 1913) is a response to a stimulus where environmental changes arising through teaching or directed interactions bring about changes within an individual.

Behaviour modification, the use of positive (reward) or negative (punitive) reinforcement, is a pedagogic approach, premised in *operant conditioning*, focusing upon the external causes of behaviour rather than internal responses. It is used frequently in schools and regularly evidenced in teaching children with complex needs as a means of manipulating or adapting learning behaviours[9].

Criticisms of behaviourism focus upon the simplicity and limitations of a stimulus-response model, often ignoring genetic or inherent factors; however, Skinner (1969:45), an influential behaviourist, shifted his perspective to contend that it is much more complex, coming to recognise that central processes or neurological character also shape our responses to stimuli. Identification of the influence of an individual's neurological character (see Chapter 2) should be explored when, or if, considering a behaviourist approach in the classroom.

Behaviourism in the Classroom

Operant learning theory (Skinner, 1953) associates rewards, positive reinforcements and punishments or negative reinforcements with desired classroom behaviours. These reinforcements may be through social responses such as smiles, verbal encouragement, praise or via tangible/ concrete rewards. The planned application of either or both social approaches and concrete rewards in the classroom to modify behaviour was described by Skinner as a Token Economy. The use of Token Economy programmes (Figure 4.2) is often used in classrooms, sticker charts for good work, use of stamp cards leading to rewards as chosen by the child, e.g. watch Thomas the Tank engine videos, 5 minutes on an iPad.

There are examples where the use of Token Economies has been successful in adapting behaviours for children with complex needs. In 2011, research by Sethy & Mokashi[10] reported that a Token Economy programme administered over 20 sessions

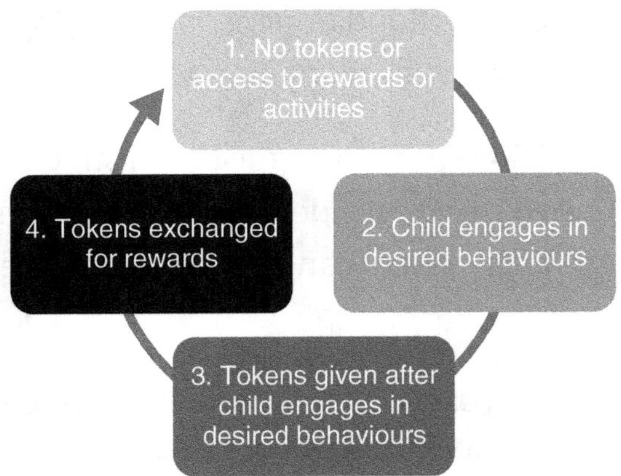

Figure 4.2 Basic Token Economy

had significantly reduced drooling amongst 25 children with cerebral palsy aged 5 to 12 years. The intervention's aim was to change the automatic reflex of swallowing to a cognitive level which could be controlled and reduced. Further studies, albeit with small numbers of participants, suggest that Token Economy Programmes were successful in improving the concentration of children with special needs in mainstream classrooms[11] for reducing off-task behaviour for children identified as having Attention Deficit Hyperactivity Disorder[12] (ADHD) and improving on-task behaviour for children labelled as Autistic[13].

The principles of a behaviourist approach to classroom practice are evidenced in Applied Behaviour Analysis (ABA)[14].

- ABA is a therapeutic approach based upon the principles of operant conditioning and used frequently as a standard intervention for autistic individuals.
- Drawing upon Kanner's 1943 definition of autism, Lovaas (1987[15]) contended that the 'etiology of autism is not known, and the outcome is very poor' (pg. 3) and designed ABA as a 'therapeutic treatment' to target self-stimulatory behaviours and associated skills.

However, having gained popularity as an intervention for 'normalising' neurodivergent behaviours, concerns regarding its use as a kind of conversion therapy, potentially harmful to children and including the possibility of posttraumatic stress symptoms following the intervention[16] were raised[17] . As our understanding and aetiology of Autism has progressed, so has the potential for adapting behaviourist theories, as a structured, sequenced and potentially effective and efficient approach for use in the classroom, supportive of positive reinforcement for holistic development[18], challenging perceptions of 'poor outcomes.' As emphasised throughout this book, the application of any approach should consider the needs and well-being of the learner.

Reader Reflection

Consider the strengths and drawbacks of a behaviourist approach to learning. What are the challenges in implementing a consistent approach to implementing a Token Economy Approach?

Your reflection may have led you to consider how interventions predominantly focus on corrective interventions, fixing the deficit. As identified in the section below, there is an increasing transition to identifying what a child can do and using that as a starting point. This is recognised in the move towards neurodiversity affirming frameworks, heralding a shift towards the celebration of differences as opposed to solely deficit-based descriptions[19]. This transition is also supported by research, which promotes increasing engagement in collaboration within, across and by relevant communities and individuals. Creating opportunities for individuals to tell their own stories and experiences as participants enables meaningful change, premised on a greater understanding of what works and what doesn't[20]. As identified in the opening text, Denni suggests that interaction requires a willingness by everyone to change their understanding of how to communicate, adapting and adopting a different perspective. Denni's explanation mirrors the need to reframe reciprocity and mutual commitment to respect differences as being a shared responsibility within any interaction, as explained through the double-empathy problem[21]. This problem arises because we arrive at communication from different sides of a bridge with different experiences and ways of communicating. As a consequence, neurotypical or non-autistic individuals commonly absolve themselves of responsibility to adjust and meet partway across the bridge; the expectation and pressure to cross the bridge is placed upon the neurodivergent individual.

4.2 Give it a go

There are several strategies which can be used to improve empathy between individuals and increase positive interactions. Here are some suggestions which you might like to consider defining:

1. Active listening

2. Perspective taking
3. Practice mindfulness
4. Increased awareness of differences

See end of chapter for answers

Cognitive/Constructivist/Developmental Psychology

Poor learning outcomes may be redressed through structured and connected learning aligned with explanations offered within Cognitive/Constructivist/Developmental psychology. These fields are discussed collectively here, although they can be argued as being individually distinctive. Hopefully, the reasoning for combining them becomes clear as you read on.

No explanation of learning can ignore the significant contribution made by Piaget (1896–1980), considered the father of constructivism. Piaget proposed that children grow into learning, progressing through four major stages which correlate with specific ages from birth to adulthood. A challenge immediately recognised when working with children with Complex Needs is that their cognitive or intellectual development (Mental Age [MA]) does not neatly align with their chronological age (CA), associated with the four-stage Piagetian theory (See Chapter 6). As identified in Chapter 2, when discussing brain architecture, the first stage of cognitive development, the sensorimotor stage (0–2 years), is significant in processing information and starting to form the connections between the external world and our brain.

Children with complex needs may evidence achievement of many age-expected milestones but present these in atypical patterns of development across SPICE domains. Alternative debates within the field of cognitivist psychology question the timings of developmental patterns, identifying that children are not passive 'blobs'[22] but are motivated to interact[23] given the correct stimulus. For some children, progress within and beyond the stages stalls and staggered development is observed. Strategies to support development, across all domains, should be planned to meet the individual's current developmental stage, irrespective of CA. According to cognitive psychology, scaffolding learning through mediated interactions with a *more knowledgeable other* (MKO) (Vygotsky, 1896–1934) is the structure required to achieve this. Of significance to the success of scaffolding in the classroom, especially when working with children with complex needs, is accurate identification of what a child can do with support and the steps needed to achieve the same task unsupported. The distance between with and without support is described as the *Zone of Proximal Development* (ZPD). Crossing the ZPD demands social and cultural interactions, promoting communication and engagement between the child and MKO. It places emphasis upon the value of the teacher-child relationship and the environmental situation, reducing a sense the child may have of 'social displacement' and reducing the need for other 'corrective education models'[24]

4.3 Give it a go... Learning Theories

1. Which psychologist is considered the father of constructivism?
2. What is the first stage of cognitive development according to Piaget?
3. What does the term MA refer to?
4. True or False: According to cognitive psychology, children are passive 'blobs' and do not interact with their environment.
5. True or False: The Zone of Proximal Development (ZPD) refers to the distance between what a child can do with support and what they can do without support.
6. Explain the significance of scaffolding in the classroom, especially when working with children with complex needs.
7. Describe how Piaget's theory of cognitive development stages might present challenges when working with children with complex needs.
8. What role does the teacher-child relationship play in crossing the Zone of Proximal Development (ZPD)?

See end of chapter for answers

Progressing the significance of interaction, Bruner (1915–2016) proposed that children learn through discovery when exposed to the same information repeatedly but in different styles and methods. 'Learning should not only take us somewhere; it should allow us later to go furthermore easily'[25] (pg. 40).
Learning is the process of:

- receiving and filtering multiple pieces of information simultaneously from many diverse sources;
- it is the precursor to thinking.

'Challenging the concept of fixed stages and ages, and that intellectual development is not a 'clockwork sequence of events'[20] (p.50), Bruner contended that cognitive growth is dependent upon engagement with the value or 'representation' of experiences and our ability to code and process representations so that they become relevant and reusable. Physical engagement, or as Bruner described it:

- *Enactive representation* involves learning through hands-on experiences, dependent upon motor development. It requires forming memories, the ability to retrieve past experiences, and to perceive them without an object being present,
- *Iconic representation*, follows. It builds abilities in associating experiences, objects with meaningful language and
- *Symbolic representation* how we explain, expand and reuse learning.

The latter stage, the internalisation of thought processes and language as a cognitive tool, corresponds with Vygotsky's theory (1986), which emphasises the importance of transforming external interactions into internal dialogue, which ultimately leads to new hierarchical structures for dealing with new information.

Reader Reflection

Combining these theories provides a holistic approach to teaching, recognising that learning is not a linear process but a dynamic interaction of cognitive, social, and cultural factors. How can this integrated perspective inform your teaching and support complex needs, ensuring inclusive pedagogies are in place?

A child's ability to engage with their environment forms the foundations of learning and is the premise of developmental psychology theory, specifically ecological systems theory, or bio-ecological model (Bronfenbrenner, 1979). This model offers an insight into how a child develops in the complex social context in which they are situated and how the interactions between and across these contexts shape their growth. Growth is originally identified in relation to sensory and neurological maturation, then through qualitative alterations in personal attributes, behaviour and character (As seen in Figure 4.3).

Over time, Bronfenbrenner's theory evolved, culminating in the *Process-Person-Context-Time* (PPCT) model. The later iteration (2005) is posited upon two central ideas, which are integral to a connected approach in teaching children with complex needs.

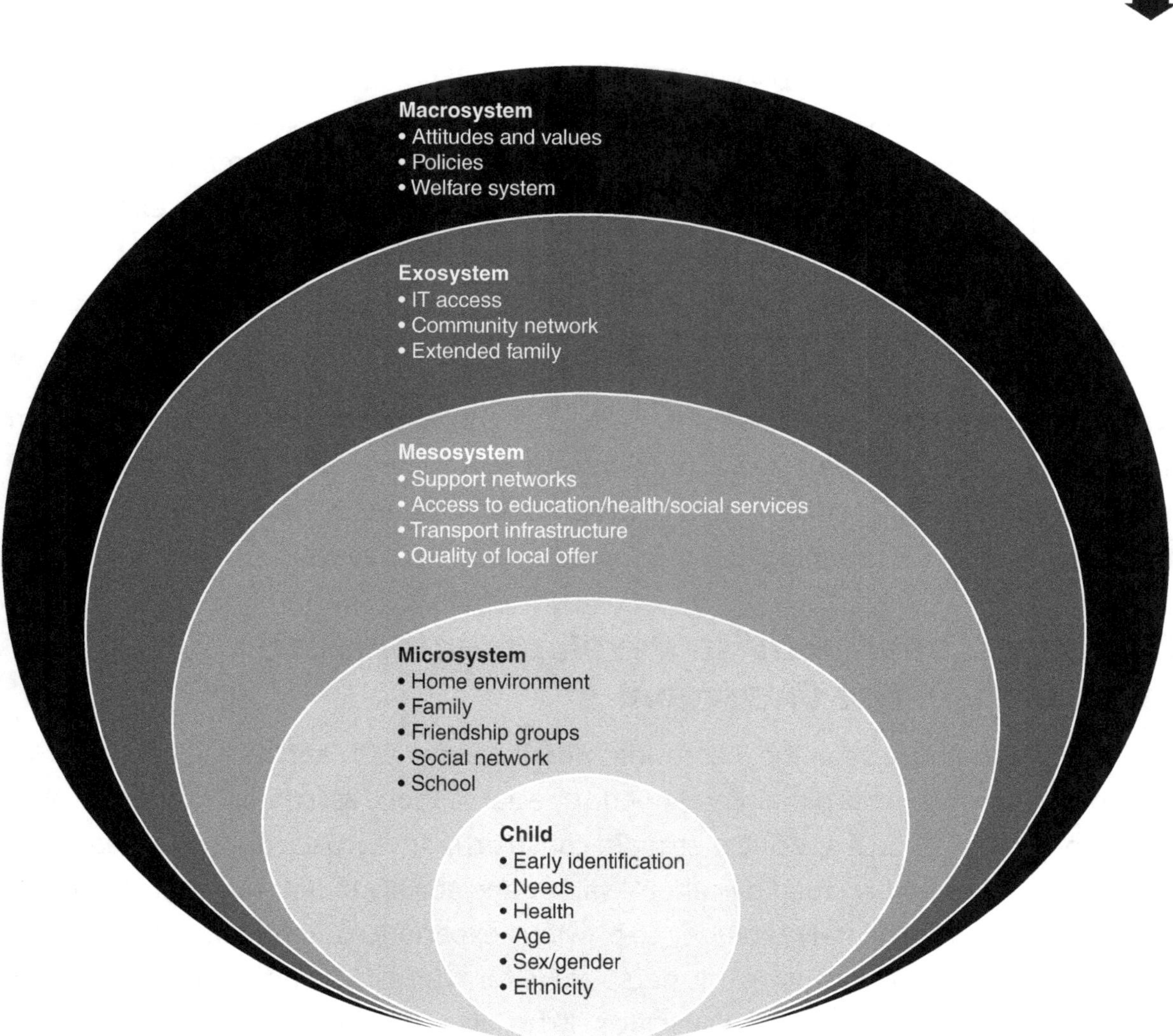

Figure 4.3 Application of Ecological System to Complex Needs

1. Human development is a progressive, recurring process centred upon a reciprocal interaction between an *individual* and their environment, a *proximal process*.
2. The *context* (spatial location including home, school, community, etc.) and *time* (temporal nature, both chronologically, duration, continuous or specific, etc.) aspects are interdependent propositions which modify the nature of the learning experience and structure and shape the child, and adults' characteristics.

Bronfenbrenner described three personal characteristics which influence the response to a situation:

1. *Demand Characteristic* – Engaging with another person generates an instinctive stimulus, which demands a personal response based upon discerning characteristics such as age, gender, and physical appearance.

2. *Resource Characteristic* – This engagement may trigger a reaction based upon mental or emotional resources associated with previous encounters, experiences, and knowledge. This extends beyond the person to include social and material resources which are connected to both psychological and physiological states, for example, being cared for or obversely, neglected.
3. *Force Characteristic* – explain how a child is then motivated or displays differing attributes in coping or dealing with the situation.

Whilst Bronfenbrenner developed this model, the application of PPCT to the classroom has been predominantly left to practitioners and researchers[26], with its contribution to understanding learning, challenges faced (including Adverse Childhood Trauma [ACT]) and recognised in the planning of a connected approach to teaching (Chapter 4).

Cognitive/Constructivist/Developmental (CCD) Psychology in the Classroom

The last 30 years have seen the increasing prominence of CCD and its value in promoting learning in both mainstream and special school classrooms. Contested as a philosophy rather than a specific method[27], constructivism focuses upon how learning is created by the child, shaped by cultural values and social influences. What children bring to their learning, interpretations of previous experiences, shape their encounter with new information. Accepting this perspective for typical development, children with complex needs may require more specific instruction to progress with their learning; exposure to new experiences may not be sufficient to ensure learning takes place. Readiness for learning and conceptual, intellectual leaps cannot be determined by typical developmental milestones (Cognitivism) and the spatial and temporal aspects, when and where are significant in planning an appropriate curriculum (Figure 4.4).

Identifying how cultural experiences can inform a child's preparedness for learning and support curriculum planning should be cognisant that some children are deprived of normal experiences because of their complex needs, and will learn more readily if they experience an event or circumstance as opposed to talking or hearing about it as an abstract concept.

Determining how classroom learning builds upon existing competency and confidence to lead to a better Quality of Life (QoL)[28] is unquestioningly at the heart of all practice for children with complex needs. The four domains of QoL – physical health, psychological health, social relationships, and environmental health – have parallels with the SPICE domains. Assessments of QoL have been used globally to establish the 'individual's

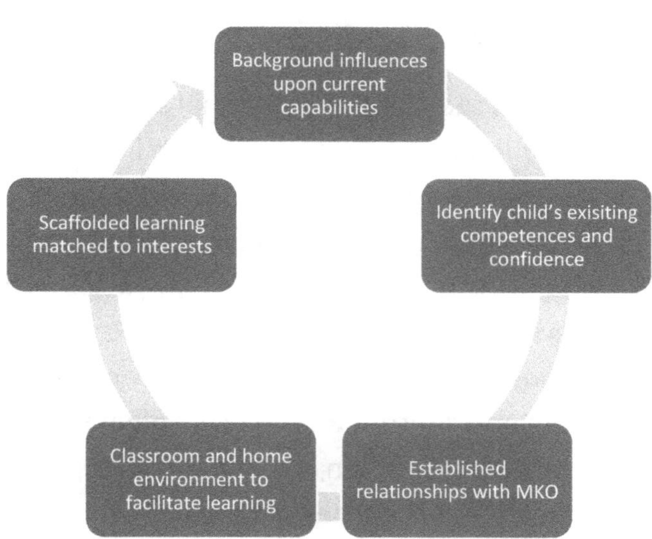

Figure 4.4 Planning for Learning

perceptions of their position in life in the context of the culture and value systems in which they live and in relation to their goals, expectations, standards, and concerns'[24] (pg. 8). What constitutes a good QoL is arguably subjective and idiosyncratic. 'For humans, it would be a dull life if we were all the same and shared similar characteristics and interests. Moreover, it is sometimes the unique characteristics and interests that are the best indicators of an individual's quality of life'[29] (pg.5). In addition, finding a reliable measure for children with complex needs is compounded by the ability to recognise their own identity and where a 'sense of self' may be limited (Chapter 1).

Reader Reflection

This is where your relationship as an MKO is key, not only in relation to the curriculum being delivered, but particularly in understanding the unique qualities and interests of the children in your classroom. 'One must keep in mind that any child with a disability is first of all a child and only afterwards an impaired child... One must not perceive in the child with a disability only the defect, the grams of the illness and not notice the kilograms of health which children possess. From the psycho-logical and pedagogical points of view, one must treat the child with a disability in the same way as a normal one' (Vygotsky, 1995, pg.44[30]).

How do you consider your role as MKO?

To what extent do you agree with Vygotsky's observations, noting that the concept of a disabled vs a normal child has changed since his ideas were originally presented?

Psychodynamic Theory

A connected approach identifies the place of emotional and social development as children grow, and an exploration of theory and research into psychodynamics provides both complementary and competing explanations of development in these domains. However, before progressing with this exploration, it is important to note that the brevity of the discussion that follows falls short in offering a comprehensive review of the volume of research available. Twenty years ago, the Psykodynamisk leksikon [Psychodynamic Encyclopedia] (Olsen, 2002) included 548 articles and 313 short biographies of main concepts and contributors to psychodynamic theory. Knowing how this research has burgeoned since then, we offer, instead, signposting to the foundations of psychodynamics and branches of research which contribute to an understanding of teaching children with complex needs.

The origin of 'dynamic' theory can be traced back to Freud, who at the start of the twentieth century 'analysed' how early experiences in childhood play out in human behaviour, feelings, emotions, and desires. His work is the foundation for research and approaches which informed therapeutic interventions and several current counselling and support practices (Jung, Adler, Erikson, and Anna Freud).
Freud projected that our personality is formed from 3 components:

- *the Id:* present from birth, internally drives us instinctively towards seeking pleasure.
- *The Ego:* develops between the ages of one to three years and works to balance our internal demands with external realities.
- *the Superego*: between three years of age and five, our moral compass evolves, steering demands and drives to enable an individual to act in a socially acceptable way. These components develop simultaneously alongside self-understanding and body awareness, progressing through five psychosexual stages.

These three personality components are balanced against seeking pleasure, combined with understanding our physiological development and a shifting focus upon different erogenous zones. The balance or imbalance is present as patterns of behaviours rehearsed through experiences in childhood and replayed in adulthood. Tensions or frustrations in drives not being met can lead to stress, anxiety, fixations, and potentially, neuroses at different and later stages of our lives.

Summary

This chapter has explored explanations of how we learn, considering stages and ages and typical developmental journeys. Consideration is given to how the journey can have bumps along the way for children with complex needs. Key theoretical explanations have been offered, but these are just a selection for you to consider when questioning how children learn. Experience might signpost you towards mixing and matching a theory to the needs being presented, whilst being ever mindful of your own role in the classroom and engaging where possible with the voice of the child.

Give it a go... Answers

4.1 Examples

Nature	*Nurture*
Inherited intelligence Personality traits – introversion/ extroversion Mental health – genetic predisposition Language development Physical potential Metabolism	Educational opportunities Personality traits – life experiences play a significant role Trauma Language-rich home environment Play and motor development opportunities Lifestyle choices Poverty

4.2 Developing Empathy

1. Active listening – try to avoid always thinking about your response or pre-empting what another person is going to say. Give your full attention to others when they speak. Use appropriate non-verbal behaviour to show that you understand their feelings and that they are being heard
2. Perspective taking – we might be right about many things, but we can also be wrong. Situations change, and we need to be aware of other people's views and interpretations of events or actions. Value their viewpoint even if it differs from your own.
3. Practice mindfulness – Try to be aware of your own responses and emotions and how these influence interactions. Be considerate of the emotions of others as well.

4. Increased awareness of differences – Recognise that the journey across the bridge may have started from a different background, culture, or array of experiences. Try to be considerate of how these differences can shape communication and interactions.

4.3 Learning Theories

1. Which psychologist is considered the father of constructivism?
   Answer: Jean Piaget
2. What is the first stage of cognitive development according to Piaget?
   Answer: Sensorimotor stage
3. What does the term MA refer to?
   Answer: The cognitive or intellectual development level of a child
4. According to cognitive psychology, children are passive 'blobs' and do not interact with their environment: **False**
5. The Zone of Proximal Development (ZPD) refers to the distance between what a child can do with support and what they can do without support: **True**
6. Explain the significance of scaffolding in the classroom, especially when working with children with complex needs.
   Answer: Scaffolding involves providing structured support to help children achieve tasks they cannot complete independently. It is crucial for children with complex needs as it helps bridge the gap between their current abilities and potential development, fostering learning and growth through guided interactions with a more knowledgeable other (MKO).
6. Describe how Piaget's theory of cognitive development stages might present challenges when working with children with complex needs.
   Answer: Piaget's theory outlines specific stages of cognitive development that correlate with chronological age. However, children with complex needs may have cognitive development (Mental Age) that does not align with their chronological age, making it challenging to apply these stages directly. As a teacher, it is important to tailor your approach to meet the individual developmental stages of each child.
7. What role does the teacher-child relationship play in crossing the Zone of Proximal Development (ZPD)?

Answer: The teacher-child relationship is vital in crossing the ZPD as it involves social and cultural interactions that promote communication and engagement. A strong, supportive relationship helps reduce feelings of social displacement and provides the necessary encouragement and guidance for the child to progress from supported to independent learning.

Notes

1 Florian, L., & Beaton, M. (2017). Inclusive pedagogy in action: getting it right for every child. *International Journal of Inclusive Education*, *22*(8), 870–884. https://doi.org/10.1080/13603116.2017.1412513
2 Hippocrates, Aphorismi, SECTION II, Part 6
3 Nolan, M. (1995). Passive and Deformed? Did Aristotle Really Say This? *New Blackfriars*, *76*(893), 237–257. www.jstor.org/stable/43249741
4 Holderness, G. (2020). The Human Heart, from Harvey to Hobbes. *Critical Survey*, *32*(3), 20–32. www.jstor.org/stable/48731727
5 McCraty, R. and Shaffer, F. (2015). Heart Rate Variability: New Perspectives on Physiological Mechanisms, Assessment of Self-Regulatory Capacity, and Health Risk. *Global Advances in Health and Medicine*, *4*, 45–61. https://doi.org/10.7453/gahmj.2014.073
6 Heart-Brain Coherence: Unlocking Mind-Body Synchronization Power
7 Snyder, P. J., Kaufman, R., Harrison, J., & Maruff, P. (2010). Charles Darwin's emotional expression "experiment" and his contribution to modern neuropharmacology. *Journal of the History of the Neurosciences*, *19*(2), 158–170. https://doi.org/10.1080/09647040903506679
8 McDonald, S. (2024). *Types of psychology*. Indeed Career Guide. Retrieved January, 2025, from www.indeed.com/career-advice/career-development/types-of-psychology
9 Simmons, B., & Watson, D. L. (2014). Challenging the developmental reductionism of 'profound and multiple learning disabilities' through academic innovation. *PMLD Link*, *26*(3), 25–27.
10 Sethy, D., & Mokashi, S. (2011). Effect of a token economy behaviour therapy on drooling in children with cerebral palsy. *International Journal of Therapy and Rehabilitation, 18*, 494–499.
11 Aziza, N. A. A., & Yasin, M. H. M. (2018). Token economy to improve concentration among students with learning disabilities in primary school. *Journal of ICSAR*, *2*(1), 32–40. ISSN (print): 2548-8619; ISSN (online): 2548-8600.
12 Cruz, E. C., Bertelli, R., & Marafão, A. J. A. (2013). A system of token economy associated to response cost applied to the out of the task behaviour of two adolescents suffering from Attention Deficit Hyperactivity Disorder (ADHD). *Revista Educação Especial*, *26*(46), 229–244. https://doi.org/10.5902/1984686X6882
13 Carnett, A., Raulston, T., Lang, R. *et al.* (2014). Effects of a Perseverative Interest-Based Token Economy on Challenging and On-Task Behavior in a Child with Autism. *J Behav Educ 23*, 368–377 https://doi.org/10.1007/s10864-014-9195-7

14 Lovaas, O. I. (1987). Behavioral treatment and normal educational and intellectual functioning in young autistic children. *Journal of Consulting and Clinical Psychology, 55*(1), 3–9. https://doi.org/10.1037//0022-006x.55.1.3
15 Lovaas, O. I. (1987). Behavioral treatment and normal educational and intellectual functioning in young autistic children. *Journal of Consulting and Clinical Psychology, 55*(1), 3–9. https://doi.org/10.1037/0022-006X.55.1.3
16 Kupferstein, H. (2018). Evidence of increased PTSD symptoms in autistics exposed to applied behavior analysis. *Advances in Autism*, *4*(1), 3–12. https://doi.org/10.1108/AIA-08-2017-0016
17 Murillo-Candelas, E., & Cragin, C. (2023). Applied behavior analysis interventions for autism spectrum disorders. *Clinical and Behavioral Learning*, *1*(1), 45–60. https://doi.org/10.1002/cbl.30738
18 Weare, K., & Gray, G. (2003). *What works in developing children's emotional and social competence and wellbeing?* (p. 113). London: Department for Education and Skills.
19 Brown, H. M., Stahmer, A. C., Dwyer, P., & Rivera, S. (2021). Changing the story: How diagnosticians can support a neurodiversity perspective from the start. *Autism*, *25*(5), 1171–1174. https://doi.org/10.1177/13623613211001012 (Original work published 2021)
20 Fletcher-Watson, S., Adams, J., Brook, K., Charman, T., Crane, L., Cusack, J., Leekam, S., Milton, D., Parr, J. R., & Pellicano, E. (2018). Making the future together: Shaping autism research through meaningful participation. *Autism*, *23*(4), 943–953. https://doi.org/10.1177/1362361318786721 (Original work published 2019)
21 Milton, D. E. M. (2012). On the ontological status of autism: the 'double empathy problem.' *Disability & Society*, *27*(6), 883–887. https://doi.org/10.1080/09687599.2012.710008
22 Schaffer, R. (1977). *Mothering*. Cambridge, MA and London, England: Harvard University Press. https://doi.org/10.4159/harvard.9780674422186
23 Trevarthen, C., & Aitken, K. J. (2001). Infant intersubjectivity: Research, theory, and clinical applications. *Journal of Child Psychology and Psychiatry, 42*(1), 3–48. https://doi.org/10.1111/1469-7610.00701
24 Galkienė, A., & Monkevičienė, O. (Eds.). (2021). *Improving inclusive education through Universal Design for Learning*. Springer. https://doi.org/10.1007/978-3-030-80658-3
25 Bruner, J.S. (2006). In Search of Pedagogy Volume I: The Selected Works of Jerome Bruner, 1957–1978 (1st ed.). Routledge. https://doi.org/10.4324/9780203088609 (p.40).
26 Xia, M., Li, X., & Tudge, J. (2020). Operationalizing Urie Bronfenbrenner's Process-Person-Context-Time Model. *Human Development*, *64*(1), 1–11. https://doi.org/10.1159/000507958
27 Graham, S., & Harris, K. R. (1996). Self-regulation and strategy instruction for students who find writing and learning challenging. In C. M. Levy & S. Ransdell (Eds.), *The science of writing: Theories, methods, individual differences, and applications* (pp. 347–360). Lawrence Erlbaum Associates, Inc.
28 World Health Organization. (2012). WHOQOL: Measuring Quality of Life. Retrieved April 9, 2025, from www.who.int/tools/whoqol
29 Brown, I., Hatton, C., & Emerson, E. (2013). Quality of Life Indicators for Individuals With Intellectual Disabilities: Extending Current Practice. *Intellectual and Developmental Disabilities*, *51*(5), 316–332. https://doi.org/10.1352/1934-9556-51.5.316
30 Vygotsky, L. S. (translated 1995). Problemy defectologii [Problems of defectology]. Moscow: Prosvecshenie Press.In Vygodskaya, G.L. (1999). Vygotsky and Problems of Special Education. *Remedial and Special Education* 20:6, 330–332.

5

Emotions and Complex Needs

Charlie was a complex young man. By the age of 15, he had been to 8 different schools, moving due to either family disruptions or school exclusion. At 18, he joined a specialist residential college for young adults with learning disabilities. During the initial honeymoon period of settling in, he was willing to express his preferred timetable choices and social activities. He was generally cheerful and engaging, enjoying banter and humour. He had good attendance and participated well during lessons. After a couple of months, Charlie's demeanour changed. He would refuse to attend some lessons, would be unpredictable, and whilst not particularly aggressive, could readily become abusive towards peers and staff for no discernible reason. He was pushing boundaries and challenging 'the rules'. Invited to explain his behaviour, Charlie would become indifferent. He then started having self-directed conversations and, on occasion, presenting as if in a completely different world to the one he usually inhabited, hallucinating of threats and fear of being attacked. Charlie was diagnosed with bipolar disorder. His file detailed systematic psychological abuse from his father, including being tied and locked in an unlit cupboard from the age of 3, where he was left when his parents went to work.

There is an increasing number of children and young people being identified as having social, emotional, and mental health (SEMH) needs. In 2023, data from the National Health Service NHS) England identified that 20.3% of children aged 8 to 16 years had a probable mental disorder[1]. DfE data[2] 2024 suggests that nearly 26,000 children in early years/ reception/ year 1 settings had a primary need in relation to SEMH. As with other terminology, SEMH is an umbrella term that requires further elaboration, exploring related aspects such as depression, low self-esteem, and anxiety. A more common recurring identifier of SEMH is Adverse Childhood Trauma (ACT) or Experiences (ACE). Multiple systemic factors contribute to the rise in SEMH, including family dynamics, socioeconomic factors, educational environment, health, cultural, and media influences[3]. Faced with these wide-ranging factors, it is understandable that some children

DOI: 10.4324/9781003301004-5

experience challenges in managing and expressing their emotions, compounded by other additional needs they may have. It is often a complicated intertwining of experiences that results in mental health needs, and unravelling the cause and finding solutions is not always straightforward. This chapter considers how theory can support understanding of SEMH needs and considers how these might underpin inclusive approaches for children with complex needs.

Not so Psychodynamic Discussions

Chapter 4 identified the increasing place of psychology in understanding learning processes with origins dating back to Freud and psychoanalysis. However, not all approaches agreed with all aspects of Freudian analysis, most notably the historical work of Horney, Klein, and Bowlby. Horney (1937[4]) espoused the assertion that emotional conflicts had a simple cause-and-effect relationship determined by early experiences. Instead, she drew attention to the cultural conditions which influence how conflicts are created and presented, challenging Freud's view that desire or fear of one or other parent wastcause of neuroses.

In addition to Horney, Klein (1927)[5] questioned whether motives and behaviour are always premised on sexual drives or striving for prestige. Klein's focus was not upon the unconscious mind but upon object relations, interpersonal relationships, where people and experiences are classed as objects. These questions are worth exploring further when considering challenges faced by some children in understanding self, other and the interconnected nature of these relationships. Bowlby (1958[6]), again by somewhat distancing his ideas from Freud's ideas around fantasies, motives, and drives, offered an exploration of emotional and social development established through attachments, based upon real experiences, observation, and relationships. 'This exacting job is scamped at one's peril. One cannot ever really give back to a child the love and attention he needed and did not receive when he was small' (1958, pg. 6).

Bowlby's theory draws from his own personal life experiences, and whilst his theories were originally eschewed, they gained broader acceptance following his report to WHO, where he claimed: '"The development of a child's character has been shown to depend essentially upon the relationship with the mother in early years. Any situation in which the child is deprived of this relationship (maternal deprivation) may have far-reaching" physical, intellectual, emotional, and social effects which may continue through adult life' (Bowlby, 1951[7]). Reporting on Attachment (1969), Separation (1973), and Loss (1980), Bowlby's explanations focus upon the significance of interpersonal rather than intrapersonal responses, emphasise positive rather than negative relationships and place a great significance upon the value of self in relation to others. In recognising that babies and young children need to experience positive and affirming relationships to support emotional and cognitive development, the absence of any secure attachments gave rise to the notion of 'Refrigerator Mother' as being a cause of autism[8].

Whilst discussed previously in Chapters 2 and 4, let us briefly consider what we mean when talking about autism. The origins of the term autism have been attributed to various sources. Derived from the Greek word "autós" meaning self, and following on from the work of others, most notably Darwin and Freud, Bleuler (1911[9]) first coined the term to describe a state of mind insulated from reality, infantile in nature and excluding other human beings. Piaget's ideas on child development were influenced by Bleuler's work, as recognised when describing pre-verbal stages as 'autistic' or 'symbolic'[10]. Kanner (1949)[11], often attributed with being the first researcher into Early Infantile Autism, described it as a 'psychopathological pattern characterised by 'a profound withdrawal from contact with people, an obsessive desire for the preservation of sameness, a skillful and even affectionate relation to objects, the retention of an intelligent and pensive physiognomy, and either mutism or the kind of language which does not seem intended to serve the purpose of interpersonal communication' (pg.416). Kanner claimed that these patterns of behaviour were caused by emotional or mental stress due to parental 'emotional refrigeration'[12] leading to physical symptoms or disorders (psychogenic)[13]. As research progressed and alternative explanations of causation were presented, Kanner (1969) retracted his views on parenting to consider genetic factors. However, the legacy of this myth continues to negatively impact the emotional experiences of autistic individuals, parents, and families[14].

What is collectively supported in research and through our own teaching experiences is that babies and young children need to experience positive, reassuring, and dependable relationships to support both physical and psychological development, with parents, carers, and educators playing an important role. As children start to feel increasingly confident in these relationships, trust develops, stress reduces, and confidence in exploring and learning increases. Consistency in relationship facilities an understanding of behavioural expectations, social codes, and boundaries[15]. For some children, the struggle to trust and form positive attachments with adults who act in their best interest can have both immediate and future repercussions across all SPICE domains.

The theories presented originally by Sigmund Freud (1856–1939) in relation to instinctual drives and then enhanced by the pioneering work of his youngest daughter, Anna (1895–1982), have made a significant contribution to understanding psychodynamics and the depth and place of unconscious conflict in understanding emotional distress arising from destructive early relationships. Anna Freud was particularly determined to emphasise the complex web of relationships experienced between a child and their parents and to find alternative approaches to treating those who needed 'developmental help'[16]. Anna Freud's theory differed from Klein's (1882–1919) views, who had worked extensively on play therapy with children. However, their collaborations alongside the joint work of Bowlby and Ainsworth[17] heralded the foundations of Attachment Theory.

Reader Reflection

Considering the increasing number of children and young people identified with social, emotional, and mental health (SEMH) needs, how can you effectively integrate theories such as Bowlby's Attachment Theory, Horney's cultural conditions, and Klein's object relations to create inclusive and supportive learning environments for children with complex needs? Reflect on potential challenges and strategies for addressing SEMH needs in the classroom.

The Evolution of Attachment Theory

The Good Childhood Report (2023)[18] identified that: 'Time and time again, when we ask children what needs to change to improve their lives, they tell us simply that they want to feel supported and listened to' (pg. 4). Application of attachment theory to the classroom and for children with complex needs offers a starting point for understanding emotional and social domains, to offer support and recognise 'the child's voice' however they communicate. More contemporary developments link back to the place of psychoanalysis, shifting the focus away from the evolutionary pre-wired processes and dependency upon forming early relationships towards understanding self in relation to our ability to 'mentalize', to understand intent and attachment as components of understanding our world and developing *epistemic trust*[19]. Epistemic trust is the unique understanding between individuals built upon authentic connections and a sense of being understood. Conversely, children build epistemic mistrust formed through early relational insecurity[20] situated in environments where a child feels overlooked, unrecognised, and unloved. For children and adults, these emotions may be based on a real or imagined disconnect with those whom they consider important in their lives.

The significance of secure relationships and forming positive bonds in early childhood, attachment theory, although generally attributed to Bowlby, is the culmination and ongoing research of many researchers identified but not exclusive to those discussed in this section (see Lorenz, 1935; Ainsworth, 1960; Main & Solomon,1990; Bartholomew & Horowitz, 1991; Bateman & Fonagy, 2016) underpinning current approaches to understanding childhood wellbeing, mental health and the use of 'developmental therapy' around trauma.

5.1 Give it a go

Scenario

- Ms. Thompson: The teacher.
- Alex: A 7-year-old autistic student with complex needs, including anxiety, appears to be increasingly agitated. He struggles to make friends in his class. Ms. Thompson has noticed that Alex often isolates himself during group activities and struggles to trust her or other classroom assistants. This is often presented as refusing to join in or follow simple requests.
- How can the theories mentioned above support Ms Thompson in helping Alex?

See end of chapter for answers

Trauma: Explanations

The identification of children being assessed as experiencing trauma has grown exponentially during and post-Covid pandemic, 2019 onwards. This increased awareness is no longer only associated with trauma-informed mental health services but has expanded to education, social care, prison services, and society-wide. This increasing interest and understanding, if identified, can enable trauma victims to be supported. However, now that the awareness flag has been raised, it is important to keep it at full mast rather than lowered to avoid negative impacts on service availability and future research[21]. Alas, this note of encouragement does come with a reality check in relation to the extent of demand and depleted services currently available for children with SEMH needs. Half a million children were reported as suffering abuse and neglect concerns in 2021/22[22]. Violence and maltreatment were the second most common cause of children and young people dying through traumatic events. Data gathered in the UK between April 2019 to March 2022 identified this as 4.40 deaths per 1 million children per year[23].

The need for children to access support in relation to mental health needs is not new, but has historically only been available through private funding. In response to the need, children, and adolescent mental health services (CAMHS) were created by the NHS in 1987. Growing understanding of child development and well-being alongside legislation led to the creation of a 4-tier system introduced in 1995 and currently practised in England[24]. However, an independent review of CAMHS in 2008 revealed the service was in crisis. A critique[25] of the services available showed an increasing emphasis upon the medicalisation of children's mental health and limited regard for socio-economic issues, associated stigma, and general lack of understanding of the individual nature of mental health and trauma. Whilst support is ideally offered through collaboration with CAMHS, the need for teachers to implement effective strategies (see Mental Health First Aid [MHFA] Training) for children with mental health needs is increasing.

Experience of abuse, physical, sexual, or psychological, is distressing and is among the most common causes of childhood trauma. Trauma may be seen from many perspectives, but is discussed here as complex or non-complex[26].

Complex trauma describes:

- A repeated, ongoing, multiple interpersonal experience.
- The circumstances exceed the child's ability to free themselves from these negative and harmful experiences, and
- Affect their development and cognitive functioning.
- Complex trauma-related events may not provide the same social validation as non-complex trauma, reducing the experiences to secrecy and personal feelings of shame, self-blame, and helplessness.

Non-complex trauma is described as:

- A single incident
- The impacts may be significant but are not perceived to be so wide-reaching.
- Single incidents usually have a beginning and an end, and
- Once the event occurs, the child can usually find a secure place to reset.
- In several cases, non-complex trauma is a shared event, e.g. accidents or natural disasters.
- A transparent approach to recognising these events enables sharing and community acceptance.

It is recognised that experiences of childhood trauma and mistreatment adversely impact upon core aspects of brain functioning, and whilst body systems adapt to

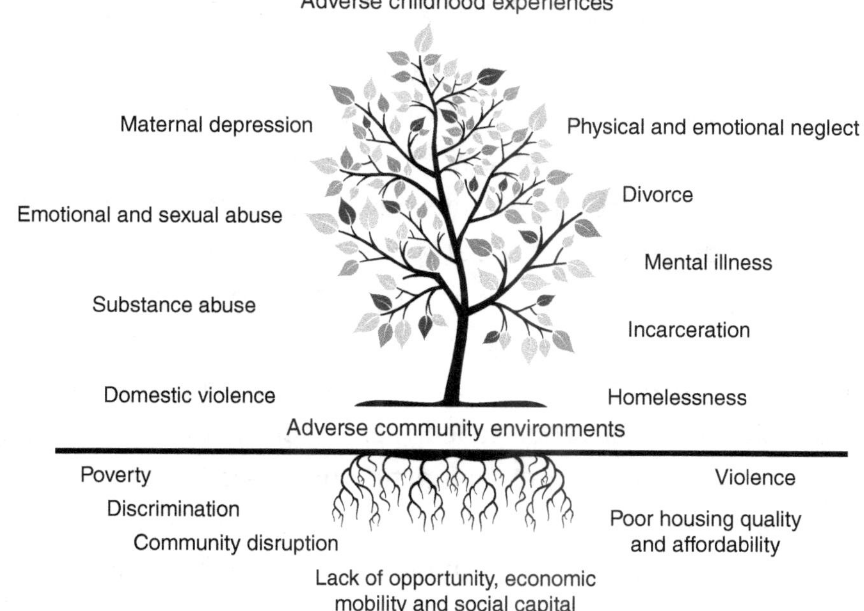

Figure 5.1 Adverse Childhood Experiences

traumatic events, the risks of poor mental health throughout life increase, a process known as latent vulnerability[27]. The individual nature or collective experience is altered by both place (spatial) and time (temporal) contexts in which the trauma occurred or occurs. Many children come to school coping with community and home-based circumstances which create emotional demands and changes in social responses. Behaviour changes from one situation to another as children learn to adapt to the context in which they find themselves, reacting to cultural norms. A number of these situations (see Figure 5.1) demand emotional resilience and skills in accommodating challenges often present from birth and throughout childhood.

One might contend that life is tough at times and that a child needs to experience setbacks to build resilience and learn how to cope. Only by overcoming challenges and navigating towards solutions can children build an understanding of their self-efficacy[28]. However, whilst losing the school netball tournament or not even being picked for the team may feel like failure, the skills to 'get over it' are simpler for some children than the dynamic coping processes required to deal with both the occurrence of a complex traumatic experience and post-traumatic demands. Bandura's social cognitive theory recognises different scales of environmental challenges but posits that self-evaluation is a key skill for self-regulation. 'Coping with trauma creates an intense need for self-management in order to regain a sense of equilibrium. One of the most important components of self-evaluation is one's perceived ability to manage critical recovery demands'[29].

Psychodynamics (and more) in the Classroom

A narrative that has been woven through the previous discussions is the importance of positive, affirming relationships with children with complex needs. To identify and celebrate all strengths and to create an environment where children can thrive and flourish. A psychodynamic approach includes developing a sense of self (Chapter 2) in relation to others as addressed using social stories[30], feeling and emotion charades, puppets, and sensory games. However, we contend that an essential component of a connected curriculum is not about doing to but enabling children to take ownership and that includes their sense of self and managing their emotions. Happiness and contentment, curiosity, and motivation to learn are internal rather than external states. Positive psychology focuses upon optimal functioning, drawing upon our individual growth for emotional wellness[31]. It involves nurturing interest in activities to promote engagement. Just as we usually eat when hungry, we learn when engaged or fully absorbed in a topic or subject. Learning is optimal when there is a state of *'flow'*, a complete immersion in an activity.

The eight characteristics of flow work well in special school environments. The best way to achieve these outcomes in the classroom, which also reaffirms aspects of Vygotsky's theory, is to plan learning that balances what is already known with the skill to undertake a new challenge. Too simplistic and boredom, too difficult and anxiety sets in. Emotional well-being is a crucial part of the learning journey. Here are some suggestions as a starting point (Table 5.1).

Table 5.1 Adapting flow for complex needs

Adapting teaching flow for complex needs	
1. Complete concentration on the task.	Minimise sensory distractions.
2. Clarity of goals and reward in mind, and immediate feedback.	Clear expectations and outcomes are set with visual reminders.
3. Transformation of time (speeding up/slowing down).	Set timings, vary pace and tone in delivery.
4. The experience is intrinsically rewarding.	Identify individual interests as the activity focus.
5. Effortlessness and ease.	Engage and plan at the right time of day.
6. There is a balance between challenge and skills.	Pitch to abilities without over- or understimulation.
7. Actions and awareness are merged, losing self-conscious rumination.	Progress to activities without affording time for engagement.
8. There is a feeling of control over the task.	Create opportunities for autonomy in the activity.

Emotional Development: Erikson and Complex Needs

Different theories explain emotional development in relation to nature or nurture processes. Individuals grow and change in their social interactions and relationships throughout life. As discussed already, Attachment Theory (Bowlby and Ainsworth) focuses on the bonds between children and their caregivers. These bonds are significant in creating a secure foundation, leading to positive emotional and social development. These bonds are enhanced by the home, school, community, and their environment, shaped by broader societal and cultural influences (Ecological Systems Theory, Bronfenbrenner Chapter 4).

Erikson, using a psychoanalytic lens to explain behaviour, proposed eight stages of social development through which we grow by processing information to resolve situations and events (Table 5.2). His ideas differ from Freud's in that Erikson focused upon the conscious self rather than unconscious drives. The process of social development is very much enmeshed in how we make sense of our environment and how we understand ourselves in relation to our surroundings, and relates to forming connections between perceptions and sensory information (Chapters 4 and 7). This understanding forms the basis of our identity. When working with children with complex needs, we might consider these stages and whether they enable a child to flourish or impact their progress. Here are suggestions with a focus on Stages 1–5, acknowledging CA vs MA of a child with complex needs.

Table 5.2 Facilitating trust development

Stage	*Observations*	*Examples of Teacher role*
Stage 1: Trust vs. Mistrust (Infancy from birth to 18 months)	Trust develops through physical touch. Promotes activity and response to new experiences.	Facilitate a positive, nurturing environment. Clarify rules and support engagement.
Stage 2: Autonomy vs. Shame and Doubt (Toddler years from 18 months to three years)	Growing sense of independence, challenging Opportunities to be autonomous are significant.	Provide choice and opportunities to explore both the school and local environments. Avoid making too many decisions for the pupils.
Stage 3: Initiative vs. Guilt (Preschool years from three to five)	Initiates action, engages in role play, and tests out the relationships and boundaries.	Play opportunities, small world, dressing up corner. Establish clear structures in the school day.
Stage 4: Industry vs. Inferiority (Middle school years from six to 11)	Establishes motivation and interests. Seeks social acceptance.	Ensure tasks and activities are supportive and mapped to abilities. Celebrate success Ensure grouping facilitates engagement and co-operation.
Stage 5: Identity vs. Confusion (Teen years from 12 to 18)	Insecurities around identity may be created. Values and attitudes, including tolerance or rejection of others.	Provide opportunities for creativity and expression. Ensure active listening is the norm in teacher-pupil interactions.

5.2 Give it a go

1. Describe one way in which, as a practitioner, you can positively connect with a child's home environment to enhance a child's emotional development according to Attachment Theory.
2. Consider a child with complex needs. How might understanding their stage in relation to Erikson's theory help in supporting their development?

See end of chapter for answers

Creating Coherence

As understanding of human development has progressed, explanations of emotional development have increasingly identified the interconnection between family, society, cultural differences, and our individual biological systems. These connections subsequently create internalised physiological pathways forming links between mental and physical states of well-being, psychophysiology, recognising how body, heart, and mind interact to work in coherence. Different emotional states, happy, sad, angry, and so forth, produce distinctive heart rate variability (HRV). Positive emotions present as smooth HRV waves, whilst negative emotions lead to erratic rhythms. The greater the coherence, the smoother the HRV, the more the well-being and functioning are optimised[32]. Rehearsing calming techniques, including breathing and meditation, has proven effective in helping children understand and manage their emotional state[33]. These interrelations of physiological, cognitive, and emotional systems may explain children's behaviour, proposing that our unique physiological patterns of activity continually influence emotional experiences, thought processes, and behaviour[34].

Summary

Historically, psychologists may have specialised in one of these approaches, arguing that a specific approach is the key to explaining human behaviour. However, as is the argument posited here, an eclectic and open approach to the different theories can facilitate exploration of different strategies to support complex learning needs and emotional development. Your role as a teacher is so significant in bringing it all together, especially given the challenges in identifying what happiness and well-being look and feel like for a child with complex needs. These children will be, if not mostly, dependent on others at both the individual and societal levels. It is the 'others' who determine and help orchestrate their life choices and achievement of optimal functioning. Their functioning is set within the physical and environmental conditions of home, school, and communities. The term 'cognitive development delay' or complex needs refers to the condition of children who have not reached a number of the expected milestones for their age. Remember that this is a very subjective concept that does not take a child's unique development journey into consideration.

Give it a go: Answers

5.1 Scenario – Suggested response

Bowlby's attachment theory believes that when children have strong, positive relationships with their parents or caregivers, they feel more confident and secure. This helps them trust others and feel safe exploring new things. When these relationships aren't strong, it can make it harder to feel comfortable around others. It is important for Alex to feel safe and supported at school. Activities to build trust start with small steps, such as planning to find dedicated time together daily, which may confirm that the teacher and school are supportive.

5.2 Connecting with a child's home environment

1. Attachment Theory: One effective way to positively connect with a child's home environment is through consistent communication and collaboration with parents or caregivers. This can be achieved by:

Regular Meetings: Plan regular meetings with parents to discuss the child's progress, share observations, and understand the child's experiences at home. This helps build a strong, collaborative relationship. Remember, these can be in person or online, but ensure you comply with data protection.

Home Visits: If feasible, conduct home visits to observe the child's environment and interactions with family members. This can provide valuable insights into the child's attachment patterns and emotional needs. Remember to always ensure your own personal safety and comply with any organisational policies.

Shared Strategies: Work with parents to develop and implement consistent strategies both at home and in the classroom. For example, if a child uses a specific calming technique at home, incorporate it into the school routine to provide continuity and security.

By fostering a strong connection with the child's home environment, you can create a more cohesive support system that enhances the child's emotional development and sense of security.

2. Understanding Erikson's theory for children with complex needs

Erikson's Stages of Psychosocial Development: Erikson's theory outlines eight stages of psychosocial development, each characterised by a specific conflict that must be resolved. Understanding a child's stage can help you tailor support to the child's developmental needs.

For a child with complex needs, such as autism and anxiety, consider the following stages:

Early Childhood (Autonomy vs. Shame and Doubt):

Age: Typical CA 2–3 years old.
Focus: Developing a sense of independence and self-control.
Support: Encourage autonomy by providing choices and opportunities for the child to make decisions. Avoid criticism and support the child's efforts to try new things.

Preschool (Initiative vs. Guilt):

Age: Typical CA 3–5 years old.
Focus: Developing initiative and the ability to lead and make decisions.
Support: Foster initiative by encouraging the child to participate in activities and projects. Provide positive reinforcement and avoid over-controlling behaviours.

School Age (Industry vs. Inferiority):

Age: Typical CA 6–11 years old.
Focus: Developing a sense of competence and achievement.
Support: Promote engagement by setting achievable goals and providing opportunities for the child to succeed. Offer praise and recognition for accomplishments and support the child in overcoming challenges.

Application in the Classroom

Encourage Participation: Provide opportunities to engage in group activities and topics that align with interests and strengths. This can help develop a sense of competence and achievement.

Positive Reinforcement: Recognise and celebrate successes, no matter how small. Positive reinforcement can boost self-esteem and motivate participation.

Supportive Environment: Create a supportive and inclusive classroom environment where it feels safe to express emotions and take on new challenges. This can help build confidence and reduce feelings of inferiority.

By connecting with home environments and understanding developmental stages, you can create a more tailored and effective support system that enhances emotional and psychosocial development.

Notes

1 Part 1: Mental health - NHS England Digital
2 Step 6: Explore data - Create your own tables
3 Tim O'Brien, & Roberts, A. (n.d.). A domains-based approach to meeting social, emotional and mental health needs. *Support for Learning, 34*(2), 179–192. https://doi.org/10.1111/1467-9604.12247
4 Horney, K. (1937). The neurotic personality of our time. New York: Norton.
5 Klein, M. (1927). The psychological principles of infant analysis. *The International Journal of Psychoanalysis, 8,* 25–37
6 Bowlby, J. (1958). Can I leave my Baby? The National Association for Mental Health available at Bowlby_Can I leave my baby_1958.pub (pediatros-thes.gr)
7 Bowlby, J. (1951). Maternal care and mental health. *Bulletin of the World Health Organization, 3,* 355–533
8 Cohmer, S. (2014).Early Infantile Autism and the Refrigerator Mother Theory (1943–1970) in Embryo Project Encyclopedia ISSN: 1940-5030 https://hdl.handle.net/10776/8149
9 Bleuler, E. (1911). *Dementia praecox or the group of schizophrenias.* International Universities Press. Translated 1950.
10 Evans, B. (2017). *The metamorphosis of autism: a history of child development in Britain* (K. Waddington, Ed.). Manchester University Press. https://doi.org/10.7765/9781526110015
11 Kanner, L. (1949). Annual Meeting in a Session on 'Psychopathological Conditions in Childhood'. Problems of nosology and psychodynamics of early infantile autism. *American Journal of Orthopsychiatry, 19*(3), 416–426. https://doi.org/10.1111/j.1939-0025.1949.tb05441.x
12 Bettelheim, B. (1967). The empty fortress: Infantile autism and the birth of the self. Free Press/Macmillan.

13 Cohmer, S. (2014).Early Infantile Autism and the Refrigerator Mother Theory (1943–1970) in Embryo Project Encyclopedia ISSN: 1940-5030 https://hdl.handle.net/10776/8149

14 Bennett, M., Webster, A. A., Goodall, E., & Rowland, S. (2018). Establishing Contexts for Support: Undoing the Legacy of the 'Refrigerator Mother' Myth. In *Life on the Autism Spectrum: Translating Myths and Misconceptions into Positive Futures*. https://doi.org/10.1007/978-981-13-3359-0_4
Tulgar, A. (2023). Autism and Refrigerator Mother Theory in Fiction: Pauline Holdstock's Here I Am!*. *Litera: Journal of Language, Literature and Culture Studies*, *32*(2), 635–652. https://doi.org/10.26650/LITERA2021-1057909

15 Bandura, A. (1997). *Self-Efficacy: The Exercise of Control.* New York, NY: W. H. Freeman and Company.

16 Edgcumbe.R. (2000). Anna Freud: a view of development, disturbance, and therapeutic Techniques. Routledge. Available at Taylor & Francis e-Library (200110.4324_9780203131466_previewpdf.pdf)

17 Bretherton, I. (1992). The origins of attachment theory: John Bowlby and Mary Ainsworth. *Developmental Psychology*, 28(5), 759–775. https://doi.org/10.1037/0012-1649.28.5.759

18 The Children's Society. The Good Childhood Report 2023: Summary and Recommendations. The Children's Society: London; 2023.

19 Fonagy, P. (2018). *Affect Regulation, Mentalization and the Development of the Self* (First edition). Taylor and Francis. www.taylorfrancis.com/books/9780429471643

20 Campbell, C., & Fonagy, P. (2023). Epistemic trust and unchanging personal narratives. *Behavioral and Brain Sciences*, *46*, e87. doi:10.1017/S0140525X22002540

21 Becker-Blease, K. A. (2017). As the world becomes trauma–informed, work to do. *Journal of Trauma & Dissociation*, *18*(2), 131–138. https://doi.org/10.1080/15299732.2017.1253401

22 National Society for the Prevention of Cruelty to Children (NSPCC) (2022) available at Half a million children suffer abuse in the UK every year | NSPCC

23 National Child Mortality Database [NCMD] Programme, (2023). Ref-404-NCMD-Trauma-Thematic-report-FINAL.pdf (hqip.org.uk)

24 Barrett, S. (2019). From Adult Lunatic Asylums to CAMHS Community Care: the Evolution of Specialist Mental Health Care for Children and Adolescents 1948–2018. XXIV. 10.4000/rfcb.4138.

25 Callaghan, J.E., Fellin, L.C. & Warner-Gale, F. (2017). A critical analysis of Child and Adolescent Mental Health Services policy in England. *Clinical Child Psychology and Psychiatry, 22*(1):109–127. doi:10.1177/1359104516640318

26 Lewis, S. J., Koenen, K. C., Ambler, A., Arseneault, L., Caspi, A., Fisher, H. L., Moffitt, T. E., & Danese, A. (2021). Unravelling the contribution of complex trauma to psychopathology and cognitive deficits: a cohort study. *British Journal of Psychiatry: the Journal of Mental Science*, *219*(2), 448–455. https://doi.org/10.1192/bjp.2021.57

27 McCrory, E. J., Gerin, M. I., & Viding, E. (2017). Annual Research Review: Childhood maltreatment, latent vulnerability and the shift to preventative psychiatry - the contribution of functional brain imaging. *Journal of Child Psychology and Psychiatry*, *58*(4), 338–357. https://doi.org/10.1111/jcpp.12713

28 Bandura, A. (1997). *Self-Efficacy: The Exercise of Control.* New York, NY: W. H. Freeman and Company.

29 Benight, C,C,, Shoji, K, James, L.E., Waldrep, E. E., Delahanty, D. L., Cieslak, R. (2015). Trauma Coping Self-Efficacy: A Context-Specific Self-Efficacy Measure for Traumatic *Stress. Psychol Trauma*. Nov;7(6):591–599. doi: 10.1037/tra0000045. PMID: 26524542; PMCID: PMC4664052.
30 Reynhout, G., Carter, M. Social Stories™ for Children with Disabilities. *J Autism Dev Disord* 36, 445–469 (2006). https://doi.org/10.1007/s10803-006-0086-1
31 Csíkszentmihályi, M. (1990). *Flow: The Psychology of Optimal Experience*. Harper & Row
32 HeartMath Institute
33 Moon, P. (2013). *Teaching Mindfulness in Schools*. Routledge.
34 McCraty, R., Atkinson, M., Tomasino, D., & Bradley, R. T. (2009). The coherent heart: Heart–brain interactions, psychophysiological coherence, and the emergence of system-wide order. *Integral Review*, 5(2), 10–115.

6

Connectivity Curriculum: Intent

Early in my teaching career, I (Julia) was asked to lead a class of eight children with a multitude of different needs in a special school. I drew upon all my training to plan what I considered to be engaging lessons, planned behaviour modification interventions and language development tasks using a token economy approach. Recalling that this was in the days before Wi-Fi and online resources, we would create sensory materials by recycling yoghurt pots and egg boxes. As entertaining as I thought I was, there was one boy, David, whom I struggled to connect with. He would arrive at school and position himself in the same corner of the classroom every morning and start rocking and repeatedly hitting his mouth with his closed fist (oral stimming). He would be aggressive if encouraged to participate and was, for most of the day, left in the same space. One day, there was a small breakthrough during Storytime. Reading the story of the three Billy Goats Gruff, I was excitedly and repeatedly leading the children clip-clopping over the bridge, in full entertainer mode. I saw David rise from his corner and slowly walk to join us. Better still, he came up and sat on my knee, squeezing his way between chest and book. Feeling rather exhilarated by David's engagement, I continued up to the point of him biting my arm and refusing to let go.

I learned a valuable lesson that afternoon about managing the environment and sensory overload. Planning the curriculum is more than resources, assessments, and worksheets. It is about observing and adapting to sensory and emotional responses and ensuring connectivity moves beyond the cognitive or indeed, as in that instance, the physical.

This chapter introduces a framework for you as a practitioner to understand the value of a holistic approach provided by the Connectivity Curriculum to meet the complex needs of children within different settings. The chapter is structured in line with the previous Ofsted Framework[1], with the focus upon the why: intent.

DOI: 10.4324/9781003301004-6

Intent

The Ofsted Framework definition of curriculum is that it is a framework for setting out the aims of a programme of education, including the knowledge and skills to be gained at each stage (intent); for translating that framework over time into a structure and narrative, within an institutional context (implementation); and for evaluating what knowledge and understanding students have gained against expectations (impact)[2].

The Connectivity Curriculum is a skills-led model, designed around communication skills and learning behaviours (being ready to learn), aimed at young people with complex needs. The emphasis of the curriculum is on developing the skills young people will need for future learning as they identify as lifelong learners, building resilience and independence. The principles behind the Connectivity Curriculum are key supporting documents. The SEND Code of Practice[3] states that high-quality adaptive teaching supports inclusive practice, enabling young people to reach their full potential. The government publications for Special Education Needs, Commission on Assessment Without Levels, McIntosh[4] and The Rochford Review[5] promote alternative assessment styles which have the young person's individuality at the centre. As practitioners, we need to consider meaningful ways of measuring all aspects of progress, including communication, social skills, physical development, resilience, and independence. It can take weeks of patience and persistence to grasp a new concept or to learn to apply an existing skill in a new way. Progress in all forms should be recognised and valued. These reforms read promisingly in celebrating complex needs and encouraging personalised learning.

Communication is at the heart of relationship building in teaching. It is a complex process, and it is important for young people to have every opportunity to over-rehearse and generalise their learning and as identified in the Connectivity Curriculum. Play, along with structured interventions are essential and ideal mediums for facilitating communication[6] . This is emphasised by the Royal College of Speech and Language Therapists[7], who outline five standards in making reasonable adjustments to ensure that communication is prioritised for people with learning disabilities and/or autism. By implementing these standards, needs are likely to be met, providing support for children and young adults towards leading fulfilling lives within their communities. A central tenet of promoting communication is that young people with complex learning needs are lifelong learners.

As educational practitioners, there needs to be a starting point, an intent for learning where interventions map against the child's maturational stage, recognising their natural

desires and interests to encourage development[8]. Learning begins where the child with complex needs is, then progresses in small steps. Determining whether these steps have been successful requires careful observations to note any changes in what they do or what they communicate.

Readers Reflection

Does the intent of The Connectivity Curriculum align with your inclusive vision?

Are you able to use alternative assessment tools to measure small steps of progress?

Why is it important to measure progress in areas beyond academic achievement?

The Curriculum Intent for Every Learner

The Connectivity Curriculum positions the individual learner at the centre of the learning process, with the initial focus or first intent being to establish a sense of self (Figure 6.1). Enabling learners to develop self-awareness starts in the early years of life and needs to be nurtured and prioritised throughout their educational journey. Once a sense of self is established, it is crucial for learners to feel valued within their school community, feeling safe and secure. This starts within their classrooms, with their peers, then expands to the wider school and over time to their local community. Intent 3 of the Connectivity Curriculum is to achieve skills for managing and living their life, including communicating

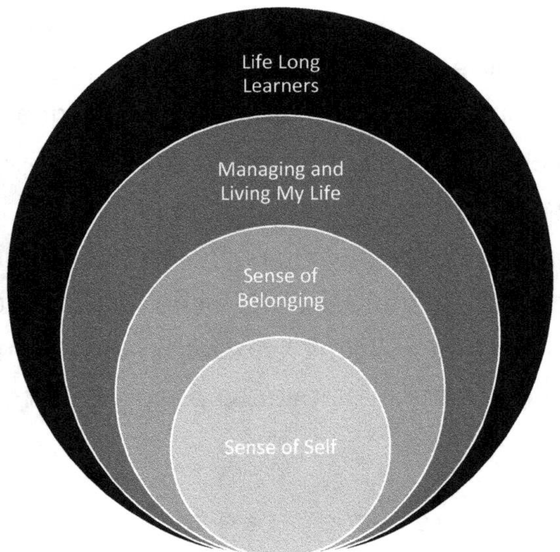

Figure 6.1 Connectivity Curriculum: Intent

their wants and wishes, emotional regulation, independence and life skills, increasing their understanding of leisure within their wider community. The curriculum progression continues to build upon these skills, facilitating successful transition out of education, enabling them to see themselves as individuals with rights and opportunities in all settings (Intent 4).

The success of the Connectivity Curriculum requires a focus on relationship building with key communication partners. Trusted relationships are enhanced through interventions which support learners' sensory differences and remove learning barriers. The Connectivity Curriculum works best as a whole school approach that is both holistic and inclusive.

Inclusion is promoted through relational practice and by creating emotionally safe learning environments[9]. This practice has been used to achieve systemic change in many educational settings, including SEND and alternative provisions. As practitioners, we can actively promote inclusion by highlighting and celebrating the changes observed in a child's learning whilst simultaneously recognising the challenges they face.

> *The cognitive profile of young people has changed; they find it hard to regulate and find themselves in a heightened state of arousal more of the time. In their cognitively formative years, our young people are not always developing healthy social norms, responsible decision-making skills, self-confidence, or resilience. They are learning to be on high alert, to be distrusting of the world around them and to rely on virtual interaction rather than human relationships.*[10]

Research identifies that schools and classrooms need to provide predictable and safe environments which foster trust through supportive relationships with all learners. Encouraging and nurturing cognitive abilities, building a sense of self and an understanding of whom to trust in their world is achieved through consistency, fairness and modelling unconditionally positive regard. Our intentions and actions should match these values and be reflected throughout the school environment. Signage - Be Safe, Be Ready, and Be Kind - needs to be displayed in every classroom and communicated in teaching at every opportunity, reinforcing language and action to enhance perception and awareness. The shared language approach is effective when the sensory integration needs of our young people are fully understood (Figure 6.2).

This phrasing, or similar, needs reinforcing for every behavioural incident, especially those requiring adult intervention. Integrating these values and embedding them into social exchanges, e.g. classroom greeting (registration), strengthens understanding, expectations, acceptance, and tolerance.

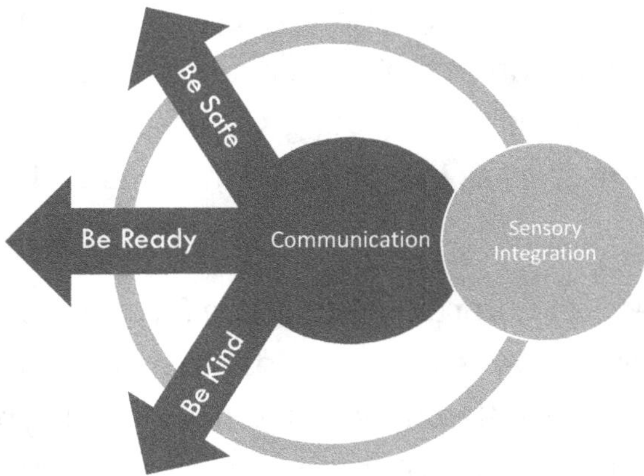

Figure 6.2 Shared Language Model for an Inclusive Approach

Building and sharing resources to be used throughout the school establishes intent. Such resources can be used in daily routines and in personal development sessions (e.g. social story activities) and support the implementation of restorative practice.

An example of a visual restorative process (Figure 6.3).

Why Communication is at the Core

I Can[11] describes communication as how an individual receives and passes on a message to another person. The information does not have to be spoken; it can be through gestures, body language, written, vocalisations, and/or facial expressions. It also entails listening and understanding how to respond. Language is much more than just spoken words and involves understanding body language, gestures and picking up nuances such as eye contact and facial expressions to become an effective communicator[12]. Typically, communication involves two people, a listener and a speaker, and a chain of interlinked processes that enable us to understand and convey messages[13]. Society could not function without language to explain complex inventions, convey ideas, or relay information[14]. Communication and language are the foundation skills for life, increasing social mobility and improving life chances[15]. However, 50% of children within the United Kingdom begin school without the communication skills they need[16]. Early identification can bring about interventions which are vital for supporting a child's language and communication skills[17], noting that whilst some children catch up with others, difficulties could continue into their adult life[18].

As practitioners, we need to think about the complex and interlinked process of communication and language development. The processes involved in development are dependent on each other, and a difficulty in one area is likely to have an impact on other aspects of the communication chain (see Figure 6.4).

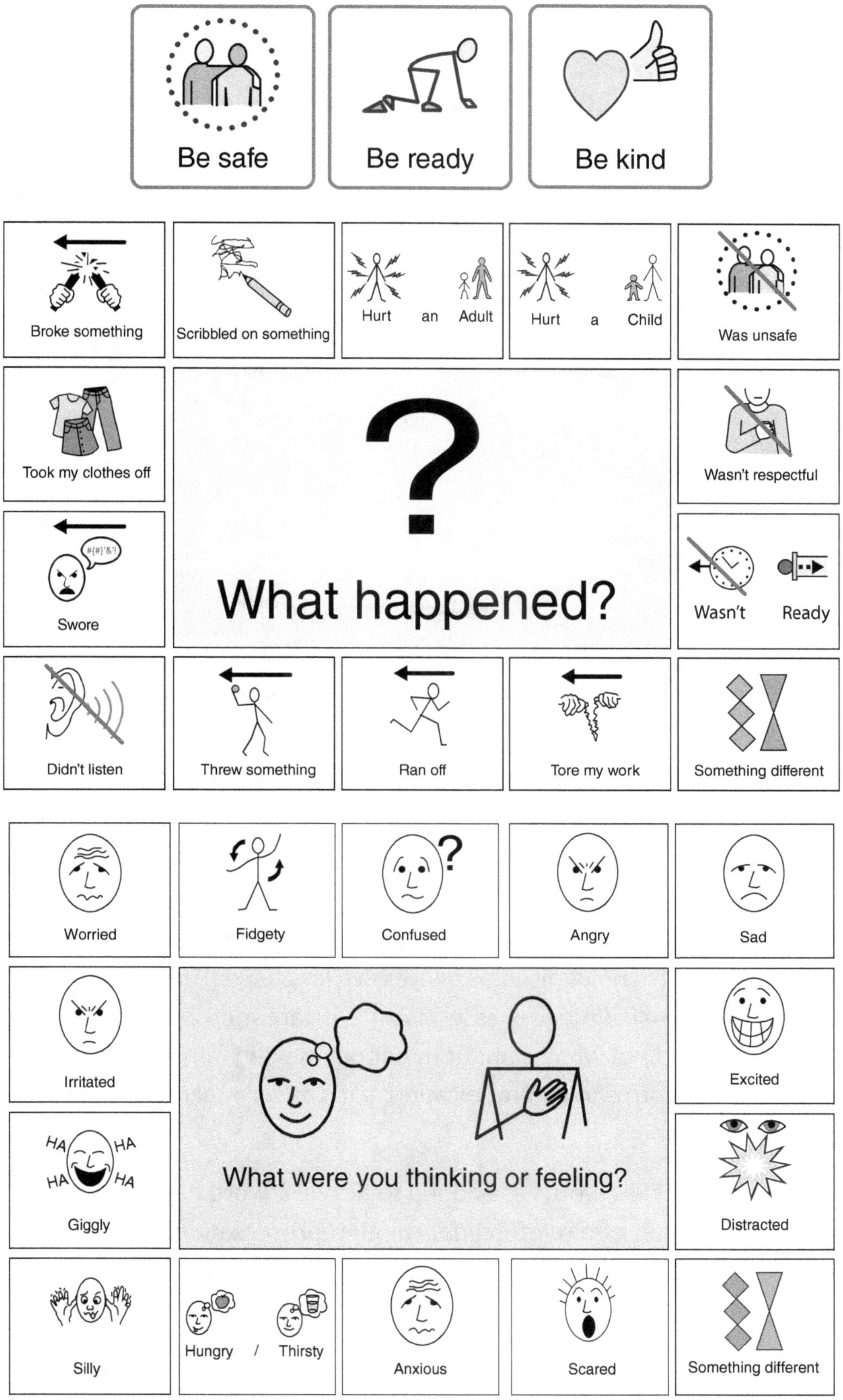

Be safe	Be ready	Be kind

Broke something	Scribbled on something	Hurt an Adult	Hurt a Child	Was unsafe
Took my clothes off	?			Wasn't respectful
Swore	What happened?			Wasn't Ready
Didn't listen	Threw something	Ran off	Tore my work	Something different

Worried	Fidgety	Confused	Angry	Sad
Irritated	What were you thinking or feeling?			Excited
Giggly				Distracted
Silly	Hungry / Thirsty	Anxious	Scared	Something different

Figure 6.3 Examples of restorative visuals. Widgit Symbols ©Widgit Software Ltd. www.widgit.com 2022–2025. Sign up for a FREE 21-day trial and access a wide range of resources, pre-made templates, and tools to get started. Find out more: widgit.com/widgitonline Alternatively, the team are happy to help. Contact them on 01926 333680 or email at info@widgit.com

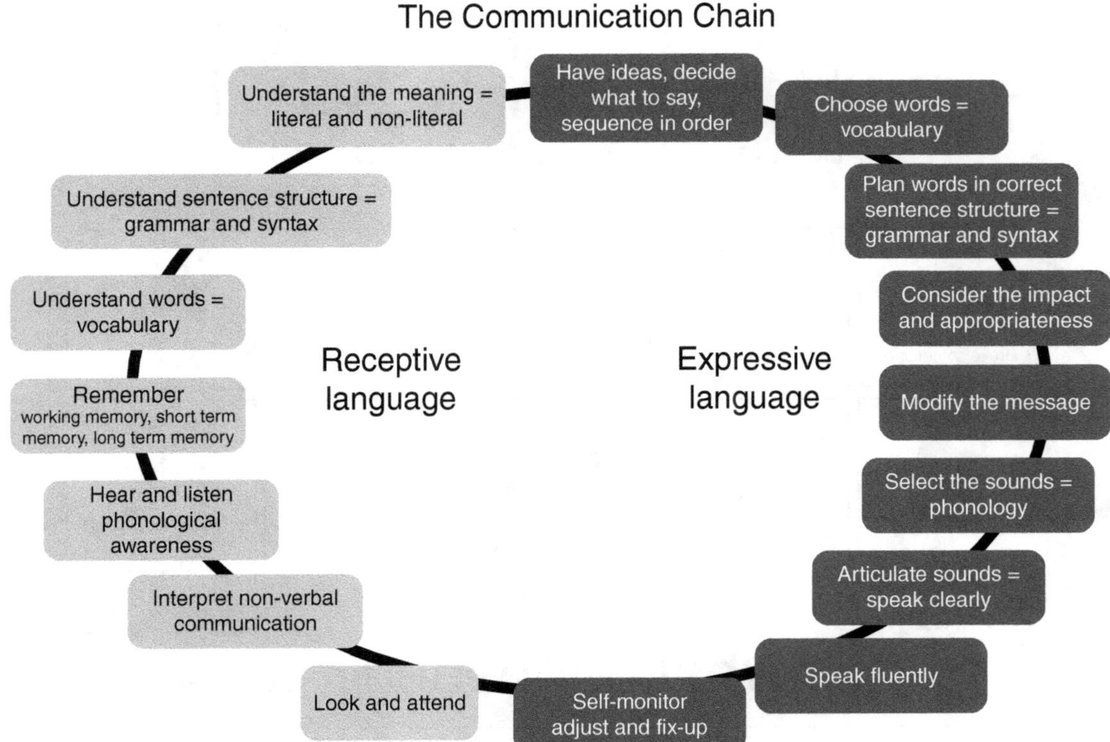

Figure 6.4 Communication Chain. Adapted from Elklan, www.elklan.co.uk

Communication: Stages of Development

Learning to communicate begins before birth with hearing in the womb. A young infant, when hearing or sight is not impaired, quickly learns to pay attention, moving their head to what they can see and hear. Early forms of communication are learnt through early interaction and play[19]. The process of understanding language is referred to as receptive language, and speaking is recognised as expressive language. Turn-taking in both receptive and expressive language is essential. It is established as an exchange process and requires anticipation of what is about to happen next in familiar routines and play. Understanding social norms in communication, such as turn-taking, is an important developmental milestone[20].

Oracy skills increase as new words are added to a child's 'word bank', acquired through daily experiences and reinforced through representations of their immediate environment[21]. Language stems from those around us, being observed, rehearsed then retained[22].

As practitioners, our intention to promote communication and language development can be evidenced throughout our teaching. The Language Development Tree[23] is a model used by Speech and Language Therapists and is a useful resource to explain the process of developing communication and language skills. The model also visually highlights the importance of play as part of the fundamentals for effective communication[24].

Intentions and Preparation

Children learn by taking in information through their senses[25]. It is a process which requires the transmission of external stimuli, via the central nervous system, to the brain, where it is analysed, and a response outcome is triggered (see Chapter 3). If this cycle is proficient, learning should be straightforward. However, if children do not gain neurological maturity, their learning will be compromised. Planning and incorporating targeted sensory support into daily classroom practice encourages sensory integration, which children with complex needs may have missed. Integration follows a series of steps:

- Sensory registration,
- Orientation,
- Interpretation,
- Organisation or response and
- Execution of a response[26].

Activities in a sensory diet can vary depending on need and range from a sensory circuit, calming, decompression to movement breaks.

Alongside this, specific approaches to encourage communication and sensory development can be planned. Here are some suggestions. We offer these as examples to explore based on research and practice. We are not promoting one approach or tool but offering a variety for you to find out about (see Chapters 7 and 8 for the Implementation and Impact of some of these activities).

- **Intensive Interaction** is an approach designed to help learners at early stages of development. It aims to develop early interaction routines and establish the fundamentals of communication, including shared attention and turn-taking[27].
- **Cued Articulation** is a set of hand cues for teaching the individual speech sounds. The cue gives clues as to how and where the speech sound is produced[28].
- Low-tech symbol-based systems for children[29]. Consider how you integrate **motor planning, core vocabulary, and fringe vocabulary**, key elements in creating a class 'total communication' system.

- **Colourful Semantics** is a speech and language therapy intervention[30] that indirectly works on developing a child's grammar by providing colour coding for the different parts/structures of a sentence.
- **'Make – Read – Sign/Say'** is an interactive system which uses a set core vocabulary combined with the colour coding of colourful semantics. Every symbol has a set place in a book to enable easier navigation, motor planning, and assist with working memory. The ethos of the system encourages all learners in the class to access the information necessary to understand a message and respond to it. The system is designed to provide visual scaffolding for all learners, enabling them to 'free up thinking space' and access the information they need to recall from their working memory.
- **Conversation diaries**[31] are helpful for learners who are strong visual processers, whose visual memory is a strength. This is particularly noticeable in Down Syndrome children. For some children with complex needs, learning through verbal instruction alone is challenging. They need visual prompts to hold information in their short-term memory (Chapter 3). Verbal words exist only for an instant and cannot be retrieved. Think to yourself, 'It needs to go in through their eyes as well as their ears'. Differences in brain functioning mean difficulty in processing and remembering information when presented verbally.
- All teaching and routines benefit from a form of visual support. **See and Learn Language and Reading**[32] is a resource designed to teach children to understand and use spoken language, from early vocabulary to early grammar and simple sentences. It also introduces children to reading first sight words, learning letter-sounds and using phonics for reading. Once children have the functionality of objects, they can start with the vocabulary sets.
- **Clicker** is a child-friendly electronic writing tool that enables students of all abilities to significantly develop their literacy skills. It has many levels of scaffolding within the software and is currently one of the few assistive technology tools that make literacy easier for children with working memory difficulties. It is compatible with Microsoft Windows and available in app form. It can be controlled through direct access, switches and eye gaze[33].
- **Aurasma App** is an Augmented Reality (AR) tool, which is defined as a combination of technologies that enable real-time mixing of computer-generated content with live video display[34]. Aurasma can be used to create video tutorials that can include a step-by-step guide for learning intention. The video tutorials included AR to enhance the user´s learning experience and make information more accessible to learners.

- **TEACCH** (Treatment and Education of Autistic and related Communication-Handicapped Children) is a well-established approach[35]. The guiding philosophy of TEACCH is to create learning and living environments which are organised visually and play to individual strengths by promoting routine-based days.

Remember, the only way to know if these approaches are helpful and whether a child has learnt something is to observe carefully and note any changes in their play or what they communicate. Communication comes in many forms.

Intention to Communicate: Reflection

As practitioners, we have daily or regular opportunities to create meaningful learning experiences. It is worthwhile recognising the small steps of progress alongside the leaps that children with complex needs make. Read through the list below and consider to what extent you can promote the communication skills and strategies suggested below.

Attention and Listening

Developing attention skills is key to learners with communication needs becoming effective listeners. Attention develops through stages and may take longer for learners with complex learning needs.

<u>Stages</u>

1. 0 –1 years: Fleeting Attention – Learners are easily distracted, and attention flits from one thing to another.
2. 1–2 years: Rigid Attention – The learner can concentrate on a single task of their own choice, but struggles with interruption by an adult. The learner may appear to be willful or obstinate.
3. 2–3 years: Single Channelled Attention – The learner cannot manage listening to an instruction whilst doing an activity. If the adult wants to give instructions, the learner will have to stop and become focused.

After progression through these stages, learners begin to develop

4. Focused attention leading to
5. Two-channelled attention and finally,
6. Integrated attention.

Key Classroom Strategies can be used to encourage attention and listening.

- Reduce distractions. Reduce the amount of background noise when talking to the child so they can focus on their listening.
- Use child name. Look at them whilst speaking. These clues will help them to focus their attention, ready to listen.
- Pay them full attention. Use play and activities of interest to encourage them to focus their attention for slightly longer each time.
- Slow down your talking speed. Pause between pieces of information. Allow the child's time to process instructions or questions before expecting a response.
- Use short, simple sentences.
- Use familiar vocabulary and avoid ambiguous language.
- Break long instructions into chunked, short steps.

The development of attention building can be facilitated following the stages of Attention Autism[36].

Receptive and Expressive Language

Receptive language is the "input" of language, the ability to understand and comprehend spoken language that you hear or read. For example, a young person's ability to listen and follow directions ("put on your coat") relies on their receptive language skills. In typical development, children can understand language before they are able to produce it. Children who have difficulties comprehending language may have receptive language difficulties or a receptive language disorder.

You might identify a receptive language difficulty if a learner with complex needs finds it challenging to:

- Follow directions
- Understand what gestures mean
- Answer simple and direct questions, including closed questions
- Identify objects and pictures
- Understand a story and develop reading comprehension

There are several factors that influence receptive language development, including exposure to language, the quality of the language environment, and individual differences in language processing. Children who are surrounded by language (people engaging in conversation and interacting with them) are more likely to develop strong receptive language skills. This includes being exposed to a variety of speakers, engaging in conversations, and exposure to reading.

Expressive language is the 'output' of language, the ability to express your wants and needs through verbal or non-verbal communication. It is the ability to put thoughts into words and sentences in a way that makes sense and is grammatically correct. Children who have difficulty communicating their wants and needs may have expressive language difficulties or an expressive language disorder. Expressive language disorders in young children are often identified when children are not meeting their developmental milestones.

Learners who have difficulties with expressive language may struggle with:

- Naming objects
- Using gestures
- Using facial expressions
- Asking questions
- Making comments
- Vocabulary
- Syntax (grammar rules)
- Semantics (word/sentence meaning)
- Morphology (forms of words)

Social Skills

Social skills start with the development of joint attention, using a variety of non-verbal skills to share and request attention. It is typically established by 20 months of age and follows a sequence of development.

- Non-verbal requesting gestures – these gestures are meant to elicit help, obtain an object, or receive assistance in manipulating objects. Examples include reaching, giving, and pointing.
- Non-verbal joint attention gestures – these gestures are used to share interest with another person about an object or an event[37].

In typical development, these skills emerge in the following order:

- **Coordinated joint looks**: 6 months. This skill has three steps and is initiated by the child. The child either looks at an object, then a person, then back to the object, or he looks at a person, an object, and then back to the person. Coordinated joint looks become more intentional around 12 months of age.

- **Showing:** 10 months (holding up an object to show it to someone)
- **Following gaze:** 12 months (following someone's gaze to a nearby item or person)
- **Reaching for and giving** items to request: 13 months.
- **Following a point:** 14 months (looking in the direction of someone's pointed finger)
- **Pointing with clear communicative intent**: 16 months. When pointing emerges, it is used for both requesting and joint attention in typical development.

The development of joint attention is usually delayed in individuals with Social Communication Difficulties, yet it plays a key role in social communication and interactions.

Key Classroom Strategies for Developing Joint Attention

- Play & engage at the same level as the child, e.g. floor
- Observe children, identifying what they enjoy doing, engage in looking at and finding things and activities that are motivating for the child to look at and engage with in two-way shifts of attention between the object and each other
- Point to motivating objects with very close proximity to it, reward any reference to looking at the object with an exaggerated expression.
- Introduce a motivating object to the child, ideally one that moves, makes sounds, or lights up and requires you to make it work. When they are interested, pause it or wait for a natural stop; pause and wait for the child to look at you, then immediately shift attention back to the object and make it work again.
- Activities that cue engagement between people and a shared meaning (and sometimes object), e.g. ready, steady, go game.

Play

Matheisen explained how acquiring listening and attention skills is a long process, and at any stage of this development, paying attention will be particularly difficult if the requirement is to focus on something we have been told to be interested in rather than our own choice[38]. There has been extensive research into learning through play; there is value and benefits for learners with complex needs[39;40;41]. The most influential gift we can give to a child is a healthy concept of play, including how to be successful at play with peers[42].

Play is an integral part of a child's growth and development:

- Sharpens cognitive and language skills
- Supports the development of impulse control
- Facilitates regulation
- Promotes social skills
- Develops cause-and-effect reasoning
- Clarifies pretend and real
- Encourages special awareness
- Extends attention span, play persistence and self-mastery[43].

Schwartz et al. captured that playing to a child is work. It helps build the mind, body, and behaviour through playful learning,[44] . There is considerable research evidence that emphasises the social nature of learning which can be achieved through play[45;46;47]. As practitioners, we need to plan to ensure skills in play are developed, enabling a sense of identity and promoting social skills such as co-operation, empathy and respect. Play is also significant in developing 'symbolic understanding' (recognising that toy objects can represent real ones), expressing imagination and fostering creativity, giving the child a sense of esteem and pride, and re-enactment of everyday situations[48].

Play is the vehicle for social development and is emphasised within the Connectivity Curriculum as the medium for consolidation and transfer of learnt content. Piaget[49] referred to 'play' as a systematic process of learning that has identifiable stages from birth to adulthood. Piaget's theory of play[50](also known as developmental stage theory) is based upon the idea that cognitive development and the learning of language require appropriate environmental stimuli and experiences to support a child's development. He suggested that there are two key processes:

- assimilation (of new knowledge and experience) and
- accommodation of those experiences into the child's existing internal organised patterns of thought and behaviour, known as schemas.

Piaget named stages to his theory, the first being the sensori-motor, which proceeds into the preoperational stage at approximately two years of age, when a child begins to speak and add pretend to their play, noting that such pretend is limited by the child's experience and imagination. Sheriden[51] discussed how types of play emerge in an orderly developmental sequence, beginning with a child learning to use their sensory and physical abilities to their advantage, which then progresses to communication and creativity. Every step forward is dependent on the successful achievement of previous stages.

Parten[52] proposed that there are six social and emotional stages of play:

1. Exploratory play – engaging in an object or area by using manipulation and movement; handling, throwing, banging and mouthing. Usually begins at three months old.
2. Solitary play – The child plays alone, typically up to two years of age.
3. Spectator play – The child watches others playing without joining in, up to two years and six months.
4. Parallel play – The child plays side by side with another child, often with similar materials, but without interacting, up to three years old.
5. Associative/partnership play – Children begin to play together, developing interactions through doing the same activities or playing with similar equipment or by imitating. Typically, between three and four years of age.
6. Cooperative play – Children interact, take turns, share and decide how and what to play. They collaborate, develop, and negotiate ideas for their play. Usually achieved around four to six years of age.

Parten's theory outlines how babies, toddlers and young children learn and develop their play with others becomes increasingly intricate and complex. Like Sheridan, he describes the exploratory stage as influential, as it involves the integration of gross motor, fine motor, and sensory processing. This stage is important in providing the foundations for hand-eye coordination, attending to everyday sounds, recognition of object permanence and an awareness of space.

Alternatively, the Aistear Project (2018:53)[53], Play England, clarified that there are many different types of play and defends that children can be involved in, more than one type at any time. For example, children often pretend they are builders (pretend play) when they are constructing a tower or a road (constructive play). Likewise, babies can initiate peek-a-boo (games with rules) while investigating a piece of fabric (exploratory play). Hughes[54] reinforces the argument that children can rapidly move from one play type to another and that their play may cover more than one aspect at a time. He suggested that shared language is fundamental to play, outlining 16 different types of play. While children may show preferences for one type of play, it is important that they experience a variety of types to support their learning and development across the four themes of well-being, identity and belonging, communicating, plus exploring and thinking[55].

Challenges for Children With Complex Needs

Learning barriers experienced by children with complex needs can be related to stagnant play[56]. Where a child struggles to progress through a stage of play, it impacts all SPICE domains (see Chapter 2, Figure 2.1). Play might be challenging for Autistic children due to difficulties in expressing and understanding the content of speech[57]. Challenges with social interaction, an unwillingness to share experiences, a lack of empathy for others, and problems with interpreting non-verbal cues contribute to these challenges in various ways. They may also find grasping the meaning of imagination difficult, leading to repetitive and obsessive behaviours. A physical need, such as cerebral palsy, may hinder an individual's ability to express and demonstrate what they know or have learnt[58]. Learners with cerebral palsy can have average or above intellectual ability, and when their control is affected, they may need longer to show what they know. In addition, McIntyre (2010)[59] outlined how the neurological differences for children with attention deficit disorder impact their perception, concentration, memory, coordination and control because children who have these conditions feel their emotions so strongly, they feel compelled to act. They are often perceived as disruptive elements in class. Wishart (2006)[60] describes young people with Down Syndrome as lacking intrinsic urges, and it can sometimes be very hard to motivate them, even when imaginative resources to encourage play are provided. Subsequently, children with Down Syndrome may adopt counterproductive strategies to avoid learning. However, an alternative perspective concludes that children with Down Syndrome can thrive during social tasks and enjoy role play, even if they do not have language; they often understand more than they can say[61].

Readers Reflection

Communication develops in line with the stages of play and, as listed above, a child's capacity to attend, to be there in the moment and focus upon the task at hand. Infant and parents share joint attention, recognising each other within familiar contexts. This attention then shifts and progresses to objects within play.

A key part of the whole process of being able to communicate is developing the ability to direct and focus our attention[62] following chronological stages of listening and attending.

What stage of play and attention do you consider the learners in your setting to be?

Are they easily distracted and have fleeting attention (CA 0–12 months) or presenting as having integrated attention (CA @ 6 years)?

Behaviour and Emotional Literacy

Within the Connectivity Curriculum, all behaviour is seen as a means of communication. A therapeutic, relational approach to teaching behaviour includes understanding the function of behaviour, which can be categorised in four different ways.

1. Sensory Processing Need

Yack et al. (2002)[63] defined sensory integration as the neurological process which happens in all of us. When we can interpret sensory information with ease, it impacts our behaviour at a subconscious level. Sometimes, though, individuals seek sensory information for comfort or to avoid a sensation because it is overwhelming. Sensory behaviours can be observed and linked to specific sensory systems using a sensory detective guide[64]. When teaching behaviour, learners need sensory tools and strategies to enable them to learn and complete tasks. The Royal College of Occupational Therapists (2021)[65] conducted a review of sensory integration and interventions. The review concluded that sensory processing issues must be considered in the context of the person's occupational engagement and performance within tasks and relevant environments. A similar review by Novak and Honan (2019)[66] determined that a 'top down' intervention improved functional outcomes by starting with child goals. For example, if a child's goal is to participate in assembly but they find this activity challenging due to unpredictable noise levels, then consider ear defenders to enable the young person to self-manage the noise around them.

2. Escape or Avoidance

Escape is when a young person is already in a situation and is communicating that they want to leave. Avoidance is when being asked to do something, and the behaviour is a means of avoiding the demand. These behaviours can be associated with a sense of failure or low self-esteem. Errorless learning or backward chaining can facilitate moving young people through these challenges. Chunking learning, as well as using now/next language and visuals, can support engagement in learning.

3. Attention Needing (Connection Seeking)

Emotional insecurity can come from insecure attachments. Bomber[67] discusses the impact of young people who have experienced trauma and loss, and how many of these children struggle to focus and think about the task of learning when they are preoccupied by unresolved emotional challenges. It is the importance of relational practice to help these young people with complex emotional needs learn healthy, adaptive responses. The use of language for these young people is important, as well as consistent responses. Use unambiguous language and focus on what they need to be doing. Instead of 'stop running', redirect with 'walking, thank you'. Engage with the child's interests and simplify tasks to reduce the threat of learning.

4. Tangible Gain

Often behaviour starts as a subconscious, unplanned response, but if the response serves the young person and changes feelings from negative to positive feelings, these behaviours can change to conscious behaviour and become tangible gain. These behaviours need to be carefully planned for as the young person perceives the behaviour as meeting their needs and them gaining from it.

Give it a go

1. What is sensory processing need, and how does it impact behaviour?
2. How can escape and avoidance behaviours be addressed in a learning environment?
3. What role does emotional insecurity play in attention-needing behaviours?
4. How can tangible gain behaviours become conscious and planned?

Intent for Complex Learning Needs and Communication Development

In establishing and determining intent for teaching in the classroom, we must be consistently mindful of presenting needs. Development is a process of change over time, and typically, older children are more accomplished in cognitive domains than younger children. Complex Needs are normally characterised by a slow rate of development[68]. Recognising that early interventions are crucial in supporting development throughout and into later life[69], there is much deliberation over critical periods for learning, stages where a child is better prepared or able to master a skill. This question includes readiness for learning language. Lenneberg[70] first implied that language learning needed to be completed by puberty; others have suggested that the acquisition of language will be compromised if not achieved by the age of six [71,72]. We question this and advocate that the evidence for a critical period for learning language is weak.

Buckley concluded that communication is fundamental to our lives as individuals, family members, students, and members of society. The evidence indicates that interventions for both speech and language should start in the first year of life, be intensive, and continue into adult years[73].

In summary, when considering your intent for learning, we encourage you to consider whether language or indeed any other forms of development are limited to a specific age, suggesting instead exploration of approaches which encourage life-long learning mapped to individual needs.

The Connectivity Curriculum is a communication, skills-based sequence, personalised to the individual learner. It promotes the interweaving of evidence based interventions with a play-based pedagogy.

Give it a go: Answers

1. What is sensory processing need, and how does it impact behaviour?
   Possible Answer: Sensory processing needs refer to the neurological process by which individuals interpret sensory information. When sensory information is processed with ease, it impacts behaviour at a subconscious level. However, individuals may seek sensory information for comfort or avoid sensations that are overwhelming. Sensory behaviours can be observed and linked to specific sensory systems using a sensory detective guide. Teaching behaviour requires sensory tools and strategies to enable learners to complete tasks effectively.
2. How can escape and avoidance behaviours be addressed in a learning environment?
   Possible Answer: Escape behaviours occur when a young person wants to leave a situation they are already in, while avoidance behaviours occur when a young person tries to avoid a demand. These behaviours can be associated with a sense of failure or low self-esteem. Strategies such as errorless learning, backward chaining, chunking learning, and using first/then language and visuals can support engagement in learning and help young people move through these challenges.
3. What role does emotional insecurity play in attention-needing behaviours?
   Possible Answer: Emotional insecurity, often stemming from insecure attachments, can lead to attention-needing behaviours. Young people who

have experienced trauma and loss may struggle to focus on learning tasks due to unresolved emotional challenges. Relational practice is crucial in helping these young people learn healthy, adaptive responses. Consistent use of unambiguous language and engaging with the child's interests can help reduce the threat of learning and support emotional security.

4. How can tangible gain behaviours become conscious and planned?
   Possible Answer: Tangible gain behaviours often start as subconscious, unplanned responses. If these behaviours serve the young person and change their feelings from negative to positive, they can become conscious and planned. Careful planning and understanding the function of these behaviours are essential to support the young person in achieving positive outcomes.

Notes

1 Ofsted Framework (2023) www.gov.uk 27 July 2024.
2 Education Inspection Framework: Overview of Research (2019) www.gov.uk 27 July 2024.
3 SEND Code of Practice (2014) www.gov.uk 17 May 2017.
4 McIntosh, J. (2015) Final Report of The Commission on Assessment Without Levels. assets.publishing.service.gov.uk 17 May 2017.
5 Rochford, D. (2016) The Rochford Review: Final Report. assets.publishing.service.gov.uk 17 May 2019.
6 Sheridan, M. (1993) Spontaneous Play in Early Childhood, from Birth to Six Years. Routledge: London.
7 The Royal College of Speech and Language (2013) www.rcslt.org/ 21 July 2024.
8 MacIntyre, C. (2010) 2nd Edition Play for Children with Special Needs, Supporting Children with Learning Differences 3-9. Routledge: London and New York.
9 Dix, P. (2017) When The Adult Changes Everything Changes. Crown House.
10 Dix, P. (2017) When The Adult Changes Everything Changes. Crown House.
11 I Can (2012) Understanding Communication Development. Working with the Under – 5s. I Can Charity: Glasgow.
12 Newman, S. (1999) Small Steps Forward. Using Games and Activities to Help Your Pre-School child with Special Needs. Jessica Kingsley Publishers: London and Philadelphia.
13 McLachlan, H. (2013) Language Builders for Learners with SLD. Advice and Activities to Support Learners with Communication Needs and Severe Learning Difficulties. Elklan: UK.
14 Schwartz, S. (2004) 3rd Edition The New Language of Toys. Teaching Communication Skills to Children with Special Educational Needs. Woodbine House: USA.
15 Lock. S, Wilkinson. R, Bryan. K, Maxim. J, Edmundson. A, Bruce. C, and Moir. D. (2001) Supporting Partners of People with Aphasia in Relationships and Conversation (SPPARC). International Journal of Language and Communication Disorder. Vol. 36: pp 25–30.
16 Lock. S, Wilkinson. R, Bryan. K, Maxim. J, Edmundson. A, Bruce. C, and Moir. D. (2001) Supporting Partners of People with Aphasia in Relationships and Conversation (SPPARC). International Journal of Language and Communication Disorder. Vol. 36: pp 25–30.

17 Sher, B. (2009) Early Intervention Games. Fun, Joyful Ways to Develop Social and Motor Skills with Autism Spectrum or Sensory Processing Disorders. Jossey-Bass: USA.
18 Law. J, Boyle. J, Harris. F, Harkness. A, and Nye. C (2000) Prevalence and natural history of primary speech and language delay: findings from a systematic review of the literature. International Journal of Language and Communication Disorders. Vol. 35. Iss. 2: pp165–188.
19 Hewit, D, Firth, G, Bond, L and Jackson, R. (2011) Intensive interaction: Developing Fundamental and Early Communication Abilities. Research Gate.
20 Early Years Foundation Stage Framework (revised 2017) foundationyears.org.uk/eyfs-statutory-framework/ 17 May 2019.
21 Mathieson, K. (2013) I Am Two! Working Effectively with Two Year Olds and Their Families. The British Association of Early Childhood Education: London.
22 Nelson, C. (2007) A Neurobiological Perspective on Early Human Deprivation. Society Of Research in Child Development Vol. 1, Iss. 1: pp 13–18.
23 NHS Tayside Speech and Language Therapy (2014) www.nhstayside.scot.nhs.uk/OurServicesA-Z/ChildrenandYoungPeoplesSpeechandLanguageTherapy/PROD_254583/index.htm 26 June 2024.
24 Cambridgeshire community Services NHS Trust (2017) Child Development: Aged and Stages. https://cambspborochildrenshealth.nhs.uk/speech-language-and-communication/5 September 2017.
25 McIntyre, C. (2016) Enhancing Learning through Play. A developmental perspective for early years settings. 3rd Edition. Routledge:London.
26 Yack, E, Aquilla, P and Sutton, S. (2002) 2nd Edition Building Bridges Through Sensory Integration. Therapy for Children with Autism and Other Pervasive Developmental Disorders. Future Horizons: Canada.
27 Nind, M. and Hewitt, D. (2001) A Practical Guide to Intensive Interaction. BILD: UK.
28 Passy, J. (2016) Revised Edition. Cued Articulation. Consonants and Vowels. Australian Council for Educational Research Press: Australia.
29 ACE Training (2014) Assistive Technology www.acecentre.org.uk 12 June 2024.
30 Ogg, N. (2013) Colourful Semantics. A Practical Resource. SASS Publications: UK.
31 Utterly, W (2016) Training in the specific learning needs of children with Down syndrome. www.downsupportbradford.btck.co.uk Course attended 8 October 2016.
32 Down Syndrome Education (2013) Research. www.down-syndrome.org/en-gb/research/ 17 May 2024
33 Cricksoft (2017) Clicker 7 https://cricksoft.com/clicker/05 May 2017.
34 Lara-Prieto. V, Bravo-Quirino, E, Rivera-Campa, M, and Gutiérrez-Arredondo, J. (2015) An Innovative Self-learning Approach to 3D Printing Using Multimedia and Augmented Reality on Mobile Devices. Procedia Computer Science Vol. 75, 2015, pp 59–65.
35 Siegel, D (2003) Assessing the impact of organizational practices on the relative productivity of university technology transfer offices: an exploratory study. Research Policy Vol. 32 Iss. 1: pp 27–48.
36 www.wtt.org.uk/attachments/download.asp?file=310&type=pdf
37 Paparella, T., Stickles-Good, K. and Kasari, C. (2011) The Emergence of Non-verbal Joint Attention and requesting Skills in Young Children with Autism. Journal of Communication Disorders Vol 44 pp 569–583.

38 Mathieson, K. (2013) I Am Two! Working Effectively with Two Year Olds and Their Families. The British Association of Early Childhood Education: London
39 Moyles, J. (2010) 3rd Edition The Excellence of Play. Open University Press: UK.
40 Hall, N. and Abbott, L. (1991) Play in the Primary Curriculum. Hodder and Stoughton: UK.
41 Moor, J. (2005) 4th Edition Play, Laughing and Learning with Children on the Autism Spectrum. A Practical Resource of Play Ideas. Jessica Kingsley Publishers: London.
42 Cross, A. (2010) Come and Play. Sensory-Integration Strategies for Children with Play Challenges. Redleaf Press: USA.
43 Honig, A. (2007) Play All Ages. National Association for the Education of Young Children www.naeyc.org 17 May 2017.
44 Schwartz, M., Hijazy, S., & Deeb, I. (2021). The role of play in creating a language-conducive context in a bilingual preschool. *European Early Childhood Education Research Journal, 29*(3), 381–396. https://doi.org/10.1080/1350293X.2021.1928723
45 Bruner, J. (1986) Actual Minds, Possible Words. Cambridge, Harvard University Press.
46 McLean, I. (1991) Rational choices and Politics. Vol. 39 Iss. 3 pp 496–512.
47 Dunn, J. (2004) Children's Friendships The Beginnings of Intimacy. Blackwell Publishing, Malden.
48 Brown, S. (2010) Play. How it Shapes the Brain, Opens the Imagination and Invigorates the Soul. Penguin Group: USA.
49 Baghat. M, Elsafly. A, Shaarawy. A, and Said. T. (2018) FIRST Framework Design and Facilitate Active Deep Learner eXperience. Journal of Education and Training Studies 6(8):123
50 Piaget, J. (1962). Play, dreams and imitation in childhood. New York: Norton.
51 Sheridan, M. (1993) Spontaneous Play in Early Childhood, from Birth to Six Years. Routledge: London.
52 Parten, M. (1932) Social Participation among Preschool Children. Journal of Abnormal and Social Psychology. Vol: 27 (3): 243–269.
53 Early Childhood (2018) Aistear Research www.ncca.ie 06 June 2022
54 Hughes, B. (2002) A Playworker's Taxonomy of Play Types. 2nd Edition, London: PlayLink.
55 Sheridan, M. (1993) *Spontaneous Play in Early Childhood, from Birth to Six Years*. Routledge: London.
56 Cross, A. (2010) *Come and Play. Sensory-Integration Strategies for Children with Play Challenges.* Redleaf Press: USA.
57 Moor, J. (2005) 4th Edition *Play, Laughing and Learning with Children on the Autism Spectrum. A Practical Resource of Play Ideas.* Jessica Kingsley Publishers: London.
58 Samarasinghe, S. (2018) *Now Is The Time* www.scope.org.uk
59 MacIntyre, C. (2010) 2nd Edition *Play for Children with Special Needs, Supporting Children with Learning Differences 3-9.* Routledge: London and New York
60 Wishart, J. (2006). Avoidant learning styles and cognitive development in young children. In B. Stratford & P. Gunn, (Eds.). New Approaches to Down Syndrome, (pp.157–172). London: Cassell.
61 Buckley, A. (2017) The Next Big Thing. Research World Vol. 2017, Iss. 64.
62 Reynell, J. Cooper. J and Moodle, M. (1978) Helping Language Development: A Developmental Programme for Children with Early Learning Handicaps. London: Edward Arnold.
63 Yack, E., Sutton, S., & Aquilla, P. (2002). *Building bridges through sensory integration*. Future Horizons Inc.

64 Horwood, J. (2010) Sensory Circuits: A Sensory Motor Skills Programme for Children. LDA Publisher.
65 The Royal College Of Occupational Therapy (2021) www.rcot.co.uk/ 21st July 2024.
66 Novak and Honan (2019) Effectiveness of paediatric occupational therapy for children with disabilities: A systematic review. Occupational Therapy Journal. 66(3): 258–273
67 Bomber.L (2017) Inside I'm Hurting: Practical Strategies for Supporting Children with Attachment Difficulties in Schools. Worth Publishing.
68 Hulme, C. and Snowling, M. (2009) Developmental Disorders of Language Learning and Cognition. John Wiley & Sons.
69 Isbell.C, and Isbell.R (2007) Sensory integration: a guide for preschool teachers. Beltsville, MD: Gryphon House.
70 Lenneberg (1967) The Biological Foundations of Language. Hospital Practice, Vol 2 Iss. 12 pg59–67. Online Taylor and Frances tandfonline.com 06 Jul 2016
71 Krashen, S. (1973) Lateralization, Language Learning and The Critical Period: New Evidence. Language Learning Vol. 23, Iss. 1.
72 Pinker, S. (1994) The Language Instinct: How The Mind Creates Language. William Morrow and Company.
73 Buckley, A. (2017) The Next Big Thing. Research World Vol. 2017, Iss. 64.

7

Connectivity Curriculum: Implementation

Whilst I (Laura) was collecting pupil voice for an autistic young person who had received repeat suspensions, I had a breakthrough that enabled staff to understand what he was communicating in his actions. Joe regularly took himself to the far end of the field. Staff protocol was to follow and keep Joe in sight. Joe, when feeling overwhelmed, needed distance. He then had a map in his mind of different locations on the school field, and as his feelings and body sensations changed, he would change location on the field. If this process were interrupted, he would become dysregulated and often hit out at staff. He had been unable to communicate this in the moment until he was asked where he felt safe in school, and he started to draw his map.

This section sets out how the Connectivity Curriculum is structured to enable implementation. It is presented in 14 steps, which can be followed in sequential order, or you may consider individual steps depending on your current setting.

For learners with complex needs, their curriculum needs to be implemented through pathways to match both communicative and academic levels. All pathways follow:

- A 'Total Communication' approach that underpins the success of learners with complex learning needs by accessing the Connectivity Curriculum.
- Require a multi-sensory, play-based pedagogy to promote engagement and learning retention.

Step 1: Identify the Pathway

There are four pathways a child can follow:

1. Explorers (pre-formal)
2. Discovers (informal)

DOI: 10.4324/9781003301004-7

3. Investigators (semi-formal)
4. Applicators (formal)

Each pathway is then structured around key interventions that provide scaffolding (small steps) plus reduce the processing and cognitive load for all learners as they progress from the Explorers (pre-formal) pathway through to the Applicators (formal) pathway. Identifying the starting pathway requires assessing the learner's language level. There are several language screeners that can be used to support baselining. Ideally, the screener used would go from birth onwards. Table 7.1 offers a screener which we have used.

Step 2: Planning the curriculum

After establishing the correct pathway, the planning and delivery of the curriculum will vary.

- Explorers and Discovers pathways (Figure 7.1) follow an integrated approach to learning, supporting development across SPICE domains (see Chapter 2, Figure 2.1).
- Investigators and Applicators have a subject-specific curriculum integrated with SPICE (Figure 7.2).

Implementation at Step 2 requires planning a curriculum which is mapped against Step 1. Where the focus is upon SPS planning, using the flowchart (Figure 7.3) can help identify what and how. Specific components of the curriculum can be implemented, yet still be delivered in small, accessible steps according to the pathway selected (Figure 7.4)

If there is a particular learning goal related to specific skill development, then plan your curriculum with reference to those (Figure 7.5).

Step 3: Selecting resources – Augmentative Alternative Communication (AAC)

AAC is key to the development of learners who are pre-verbal or have a language disorder. It is important to achieve the fundamentals of communication, progressing from pre-intentional communication to intentional communication. Symbol exchange can facilitate bridging to intentional communication, where a learner exchanges a symbol in return for an item. Learners with complex needs will start with a low-tech communication system like symbol-based boards/books or an e-tran frame for eye pointing. As learners progress in their vocabulary, expand reasons for communicating, and develop their motor-planning, they can then advance to a high-tech voice output

Table 7.1 Screening Language (Markers) for the Pathways

Explorers (Pre-formal) Birth – 18 months language levels.	Auditory Comprehension Turns head towards source of sound. Anticipates event or signal. Understands a word or phrase. Jointly attends. Begins to identify familiar objects. Understands purpose of objects (cup, spoon, bed).	Expressive Communication Vocalises for pleasure and displeasure. Communicates non-verbally. Initiates a game or social routine. Vocabulary of at least one word.
Discoverers (Informal) 18 months to three years language levels.	Auditory Comprehension Follows simple instruction within everyday routines. Understands verbs in context (eat, drink, sleep). Understands spatial concepts (in, off, out of). Understands quantity concepts (one, some, rest, all). Understands descriptive concepts (big, small, wet). Understands pronouns.	Expressive Communication Vocalises for pleasure and displeasure. Communicates non-verbally. Initiates a game or social routine. Vocabulary of at least ten words. Names familiar objects. Express negatives. Combines three words (including a pronoun). Answers what and where questions. Uses verbs. **Augmentative Alternative Communication can be used to achieve these outcomes.**
Investigators (Semi-formal) 3 years to 5 years	Auditory Comprehension Groups objects. Understands negatives. Compares objects. Understands descriptive concepts (heavy, empty, same, different). Makes inferences. Understands spatial concepts (under, behind, next to, in front of). Understands time concepts (night, day). Understands quantity concepts (to five). Follows complex instructions.	Expressive Communication Describes a procedure. Able to categorise. Combines four words (including a pronoun). Answers when and how questions. Uses prepositions. **Augmentative Alternative Communication can be used to achieve these outcomes.**
Applicators (Formal) 5 years and beyond.	Auditory Comprehension Understands nouns and two modifying adjectives. Add and subtract numbers to five. Understands time/sequence concepts (last, first, autumn, summer). Understands quantity concepts (whole, half).	Expressive Communication Defines words. Builds sentences. Uses words to express quantity. Uses comparative and superlative language. Retells an event or story. Uses irregular plurals. Answers why questions **Augmentative Alternative Communication can be used to achieve these outcomes.**

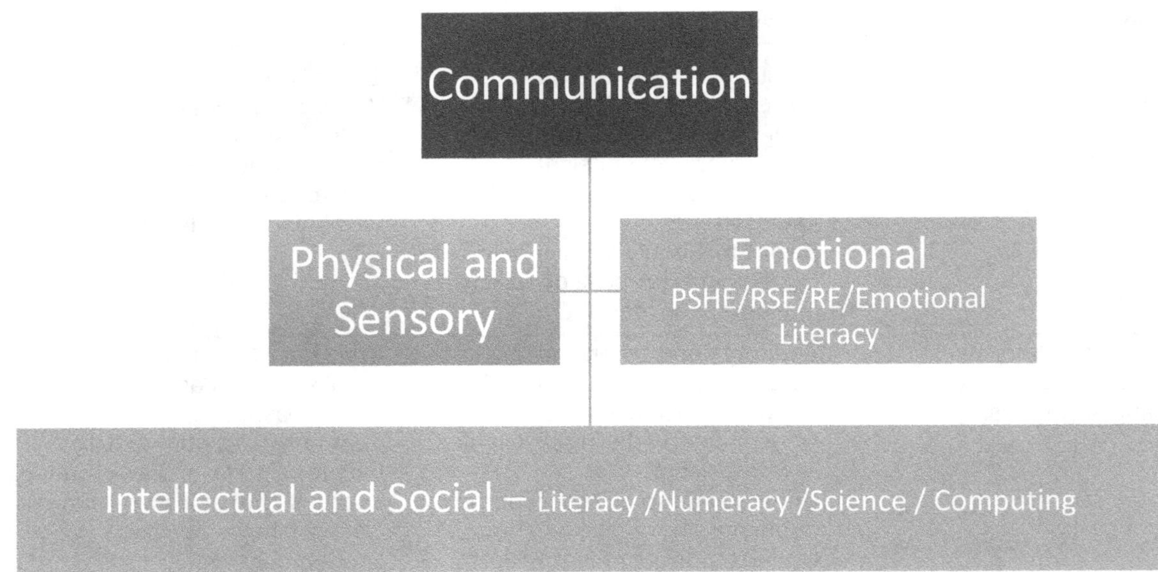

Figure 7.1 Explorer and Discovery Pathway

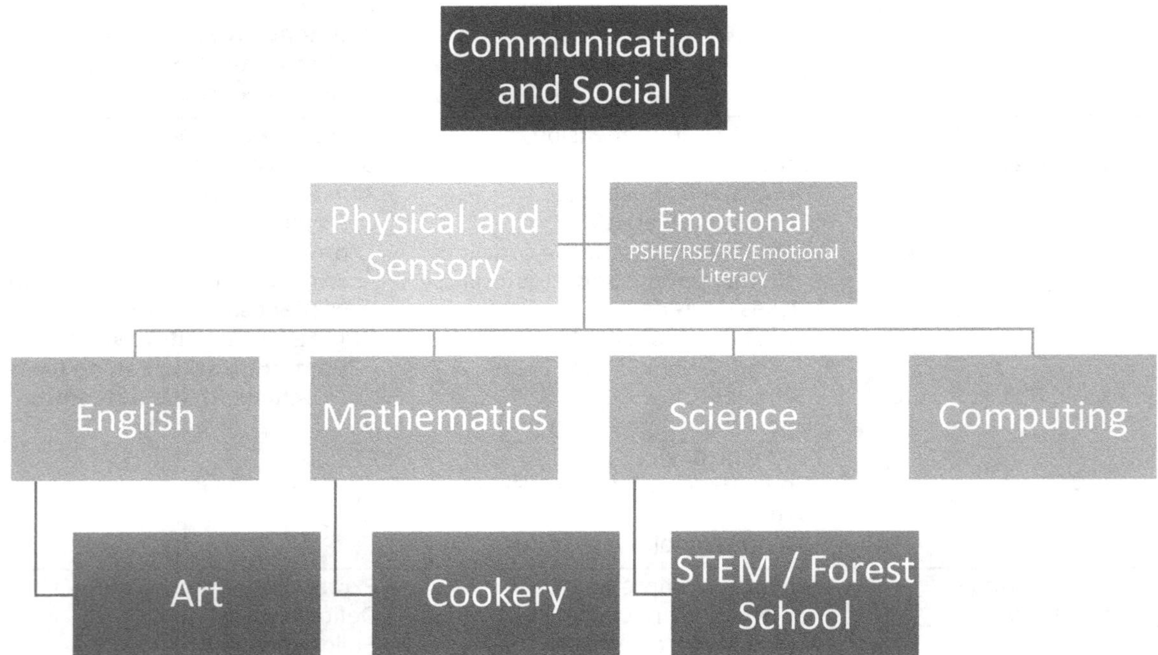

Figure 7.2 Investigators and Applicators Pathway

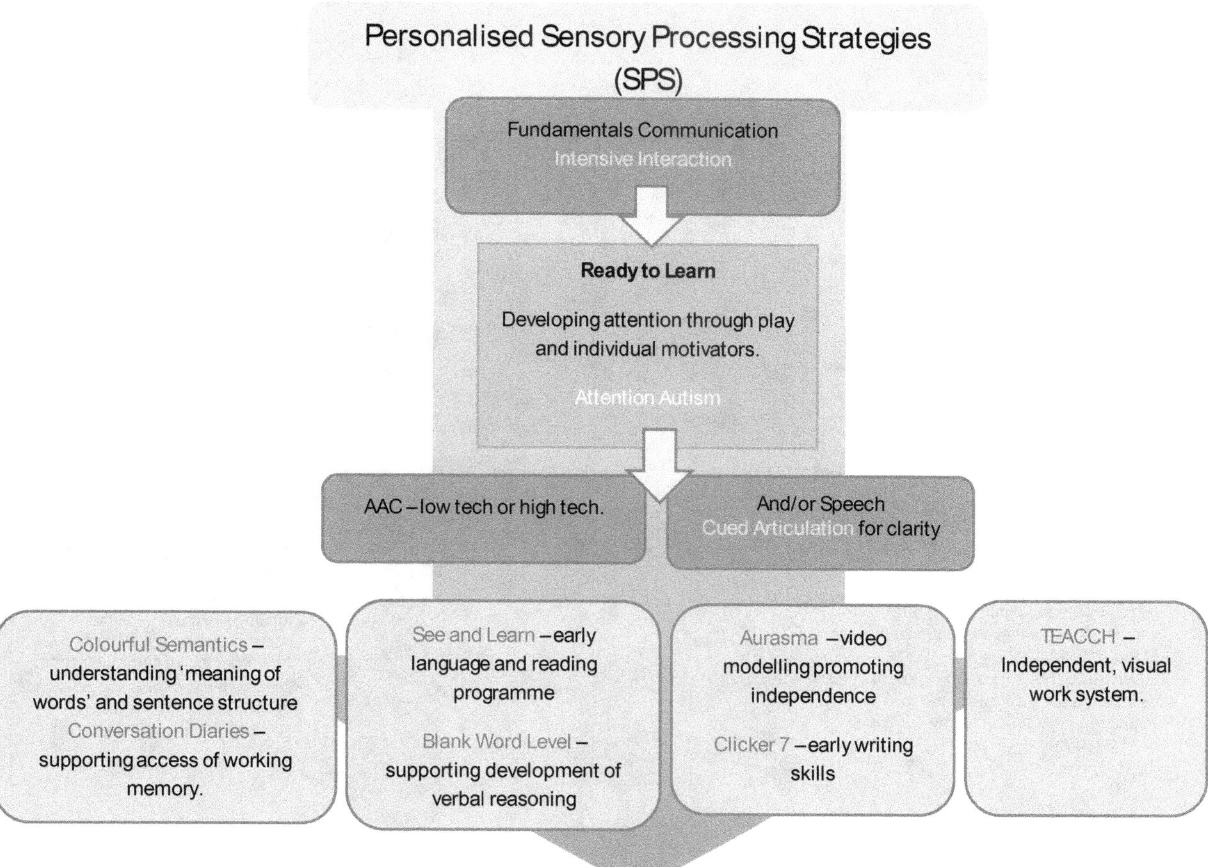

Figure 7.3 Implementation Process

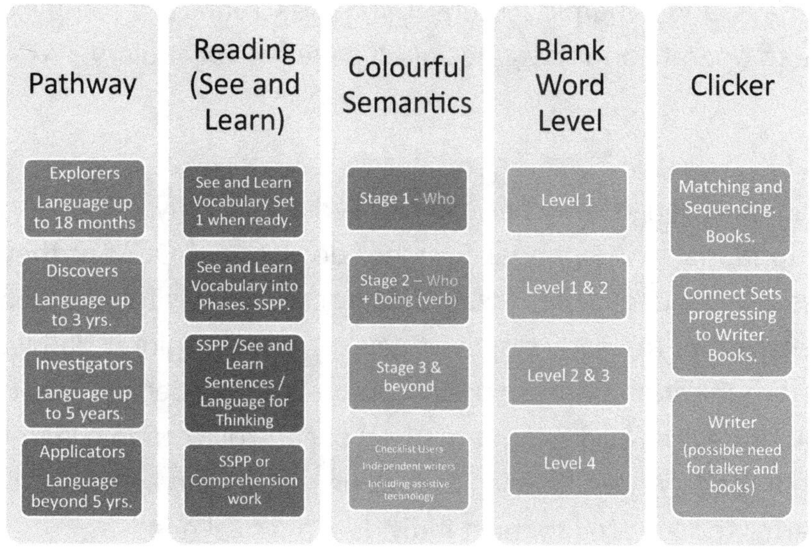

Figure 7.4 Literacy Development Implementation

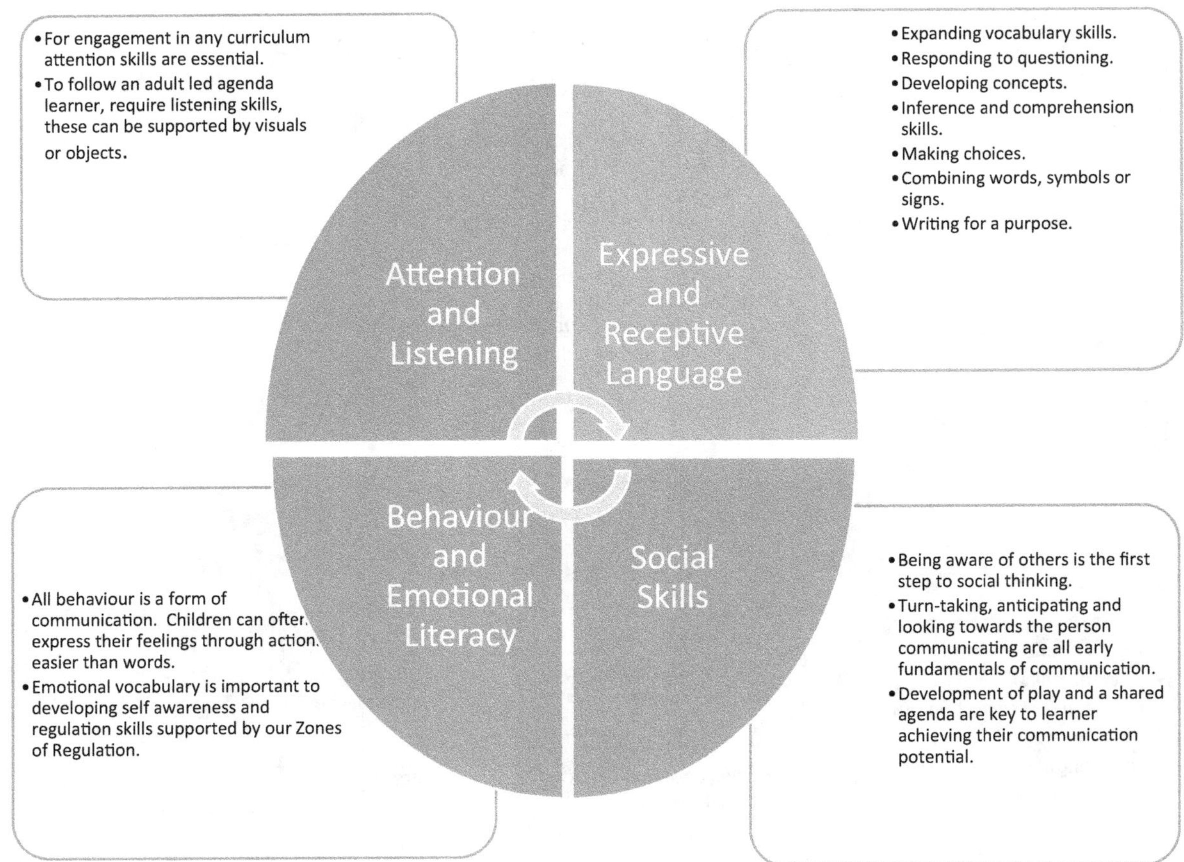

Figure 7.5 Areas of Communication

communication aid (VOCAs). There is a large range of VOCAs from single message recordings, overlays, and dynamic screens. Dynamic screens are complex, and learners need to be able to operate and navigate linked pages of vocabulary.

Switches

Similarly to symbol exchange, switches can be used at the early stages of communication to bridge pre-intentional to intentional. Switches do class as VOCAs as they can have single messages or a sequence of messages. They can support the development of cause and effect for learners at the early stages of development (Explorer pathway). They are important in communication because they promote independence. They can also be connected to other devices as the input method of control to enable learners to scan. Switches can be fitted to wheelchairs so the young person can activate them via their head, hand or arm, and leg area to meet individual physical needs.

Communication partners can be defined as anyone who communicates with the AAC user using their AAC system. Partners are not only limited to the AAC user's parent or immediate caregiver; it extends to any individuals they may interact with at home,

school or out in the community. The literature and evidence-based research suggest that communication partner involvement is directly related to positive results for the AAC user's communication skills and will reduce the likelihood of abandonment. Modelling is the key strategy for communication partners. AAC users need to see what it looks like to communicate with their AAC systems in real contexts. To do this, we need to talk to them using their AAC. Model regularly and consistently. Model across different contexts and environments. Model a wide range of communication functions.

Model the key words in the sentence. Use a slow pace as we show the AAC. Use self-talk as we model. Talk about what we are doing and what folders we are opening to find the word.

The use of AAC is closely related to the language and motor capabilities of the learners. Before introducing and implementing learning using AAC, consider interests, competency and capability. A framework to help determine this is presented in Figure 7.6.

Stages to High-tech Communication Aids for Pre-verbal/Non-verbal Learners

Figure 7.6 Augmentative Alternative Communication Progression

Step 4: Small Steps to Encourage Engagement

A graduated approach to managing behaviour is important. Having a shared understanding of the meaning behind the language used in the classroom helps shape responses supporting learners with complex needs. The same instructions and language should be used by all teaching staff – the MKO.
The graduated approach to communicating with meaning can include:

- Positive Phrasing (Focus on what the young person needs to be doing, 'stand next to me, thank you').
- Limited Choices (Give the young person an element of control within the key instruction, 'Are you going to sit on the cushion or bean bag?')
- Disempowering behaviour (planned ignore, having a 'ready to learn' break and instructing them to listen from where they are).
- And consistent scripts to support de-escalation (I am here to help. Talk and I will listen)[1].

Teaching behaviour is key in the Connectivity Curriculum. Dix[2] is an advocate for natural and educational consequences rather than a punitive system of removal and detention. When teaching behaviour, there are key components.

- Relational practice
- Role modelling unconditional positive regard with warmth and forgiveness.
- Consistency
- Scripts and routines
- Logical consequences

Natural and educational consequences can take the form of completing tasks, rehearsing, assisting with repairs, research, and restorative conversations. Protective consequences are the removal of freedom to reduce the risk of harm. Protective consequences can be increasing the staff ratio, managed use of outside space with peers, escorted in transitions and differentiated teaching spaces. Wadham clarifies that protective consequences should not happen in isolation; they should always be accompanied by an educational consequence.

Restorative conversations should be completed after every behavioural incident. The purpose is to reflect, repair, and restore by revisiting the events with a young person when they are calm, relaxed and reflective. Having a visual scaffold to assist the process is beneficial for staff to be consistent and allows the young person to feel safe within the process.

Step 5: Interoception

The Connectivity Curriculum promotes the teaching of interoception as part of meeting sensory and self-regulation needs. Mahler[3] explains the importance of teaching interoception because it is the ability to notice and connect bodily sensations with emotions. Mahler states that interoception is a significant factor in the development of effective self-regulation skills within children, teens, and adults (see Figure 7.7). Many people who experience challenges with self-regulation have underlying interoception differences. These interoceptive differences are very common in a variety of individuals, including those with autism, trauma disorders, sensory processing disorders, and anxiety. Some learners with complex needs may experience interoceptive signals that are so strong, they are immediately overwhelmed and confused. Others experience dulled or muted interoception signals, which leave them unable to respond to emotions until they reach a fever pitch. This can lead to significant difficulties with emotional regulation. Assessing a learner's interoception, awakened, and management can be completed using Table 7.2.

Step 6: Zones of Regulation

Zones of Regulation[4] is a reputable, systematic, and cognitive behavioural approach used to teach self-regulation by categorising all the different ways we feel within four coloured zones (As seen in Figure 7.8).

The Zones of Regulation curriculum provides strategies to teach learners to have increased self-awareness of ways to support managing responses, impulses, sensory differences, and improve their ability to problem solve conflicts. Zones of Regulation

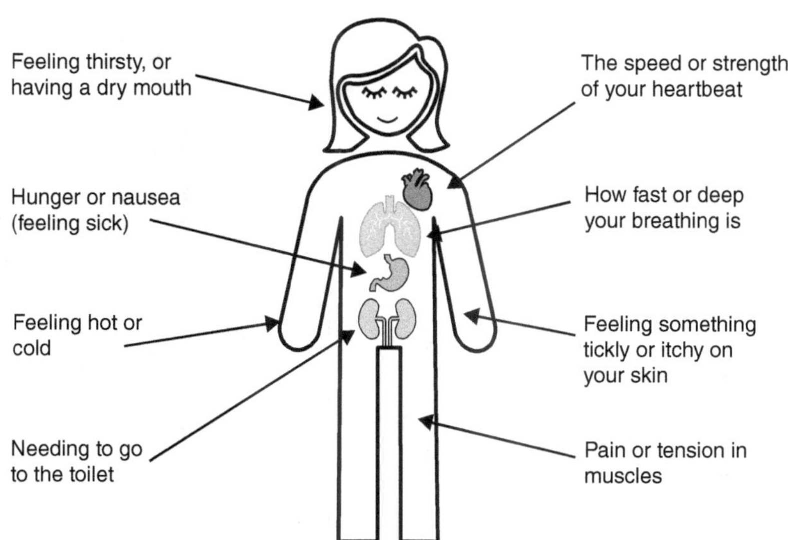

Figure 7.7 Interoception

Table 7.2 Awareness of Interoception

1. Interoception – Stage 1 My Body						
		Emerging	*Gaining*	*Mastered*	*Generalised*	*Comment*
1	Hands and Fingers					
2	Feet and Toes					
3	Mouth					
4	Eyes					
5	Ears					
6	Nose					
7	Voice					
8	Cheeks					
9	Skin					
10	Muscle					
11	Lungs					
12	Heart					
13	Brain and Head					
14	Stomach					
15	Bladder					
16	Body Scan Map					
Interoception – Stage 2 My Emotions						
		Emerging	*Gaining*	*Mastered*	*Generalised*	*Comment*
17	I can link body clues to emotions					
18	I can identify the body changes for named emotions.					
19	I can identify the cause of changes in my body signals.					
20	I can scale body changes linked to emotions.					
Interoception – Stage 3 My Actions						
		Emerging	*Gaining*	*Mastered*	*Generalised*	*Comment*
21	I can identify feelings linked to different body parts in the moment.					
22	I can change the way my body feels.					
23	I can change the way my body feels when it is uncomfortable.					
24	I can use a feel-good menu.					
25	I can practice making my body feel good.					

Table 7.3 Zones of Regulation Progression

Zones of Regulation – Stage 1 Exploring the Zones						
		Emerging	*Gaining*	*Mastered*	*Generalised*	*Comment*
1	Introduce Zones of Regulation					
2	Explore Green Zone					
3	Explore Blue Zone					
4	Explore Yellow Zone					
5	Explore Red Zone					
6	Know Your Zones					
Zones of Regulation – Stage 2 Zones and My Tools						
		Emerging	*Gaining*	*Mastered*	*Generalised*	*Comment*
7	Categorise Emotions into Zones					
8	Expected vs Unexpected Behaviours					
9	Identify Feelings in Others					
10	The Zones in Me					
11	Me in My Zones					
12	Explore Sensory Support Tools					
13	Explore Tools for Calming					
14	Explore Tools for Thinking					
15	My Toolkit					

will facilitate restorative conversations, which enable staff to model empathy and allow children the opportunity to resolve conflict. Importantly, Zones of Regulation (see Table 7.3) complements the interoception to support teaching cause and effect of behaviour.

Key action points are:

- We do not label a zone as good or bad.
- A child can be in more than one zone.
- Manage the zone; do not try to force them into another zone.
- Individualise the tools where possible.
- All the zones are expected at one time or another.
- It is a teaching tool, not a behavioural approach.

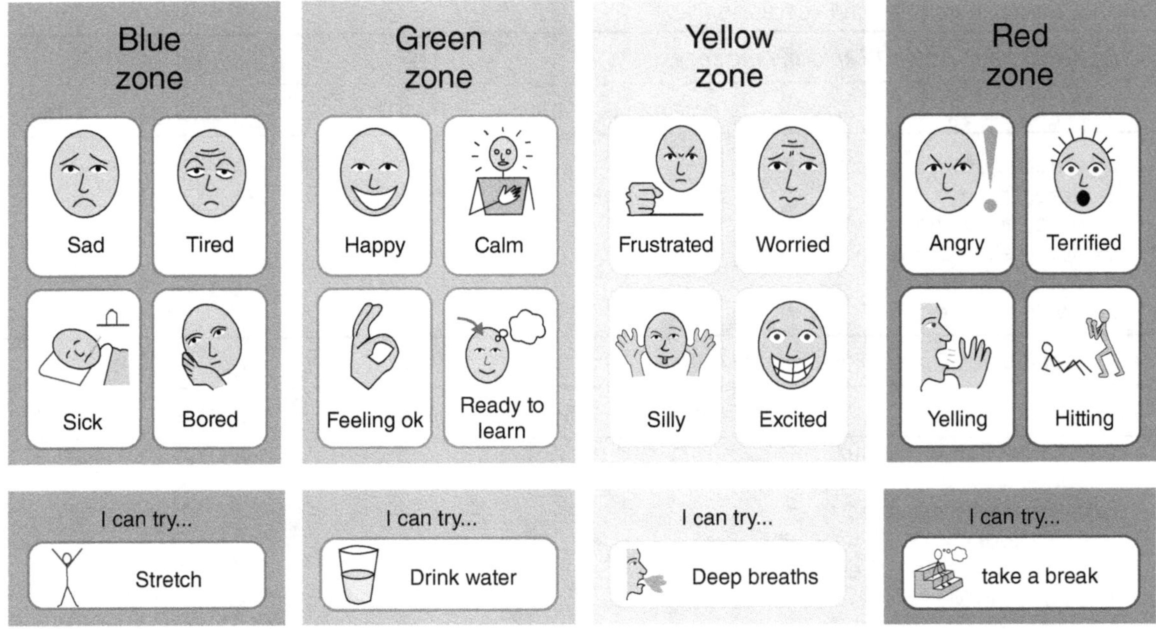

Figure 7.8 Zones of Regulation Visual

Step 7: Learning to Communicate

Learners with complex needs learn to communicate when they have a means of communicating, opportunities to communicate, and reasons to communicate. Your planning should evidence ways of implementing specific strategies mapped against the stage the learner is currently communicating at (Figure 7.9).

Their communication partner needs to be responsive to all their efforts to communicate (Figure 7.10).

Communication is most likely to occur when we are engaged, interested, and motivated. This is true whether we speak or use AAC. Everyone needs a reason to communicate: Children are unlikely to communicate unless they really want to and are motivated otherwise; there is simply no point. The basic needs are usually the first reasons for learners to communicate; expressing feelings, being tired, hungry, thirsty, or poorly. Learners then progress to indicate wants and needs by making requests, choices, rejecting items, or to gain attention. This typically happens before learners communicate for social reasons; to greet, instruct, comment, ask questions, or for the pleasure of chatting, forming relationships, and sharing information.

Motivation is key, so keeping a list of things that the AAC user likes or does not like, accompanied by resources to promote communication through play. Use motivators to plan interesting and engaging activities to give them the incentive to communicate real messages: facilitate a desire to request, choose or comment. Try to avoid using

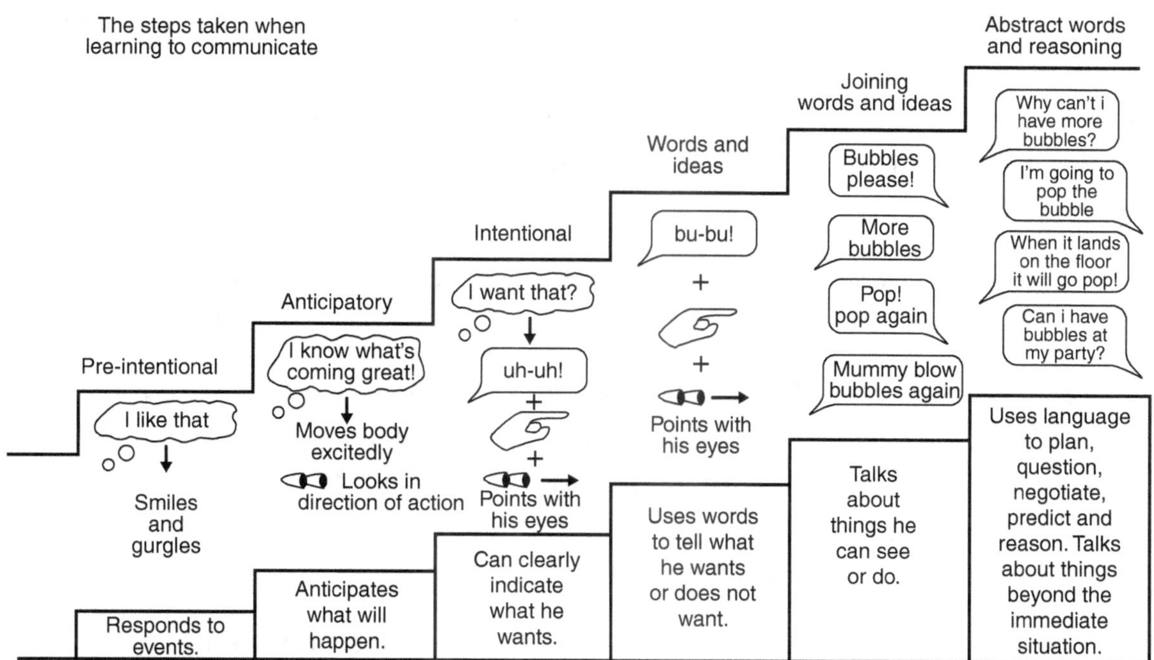

Figure 7.9 Learning to Communicate (adapted from McLachlan, 2013)

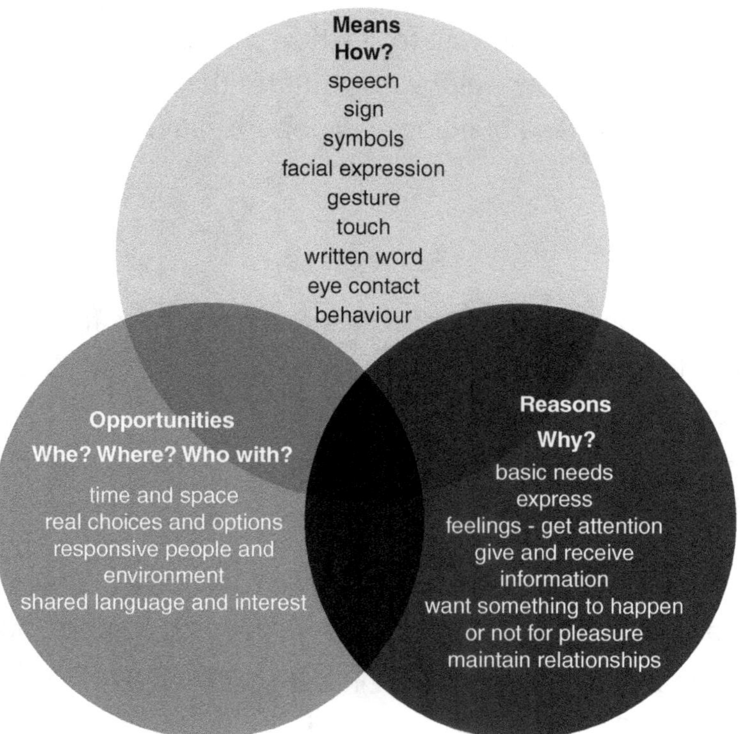

Figure 7.10 Opportunities, Means and Reasons Model, adapted from Money and Thurman (1994)[10]

AAC for boring and repetitive drill exercises. The aim is for learners to see the value and strength of the language. It is essential that we personalise children's AAC systems so that they have access to the vocabulary that they want and need, then plan for their AAC throughout the day. Look at routines and plan for where, when and how AAC can be integrated into the day.

Communication is always happening. This means there are always opportunities for modelling, interacting and building language.

Incorporate AAC into everyday routines. Routines can be an easy place to start, as often, the language and communication are predictable and familiar. Do not be afraid to shake routines up now and then. Lots of engagement and commenting can happen when things do not quite go to plan or are done differently. Use sabotage, an element of surprise, and leave a pause for a response.

Communication partners need to try not to anticipate the learners' wants and needs. Reflect on routines, and if they happen repetitively, try not to miss an opportunity for the learner to communicate what should happen. For example, if every day, the staff turn the whiteboard on ready for registration, one morning, leave it off; put the remote somewhere accessible and wait to see how they communicate within that familiar routine. It is through these everyday routines that you can reflect on with the aim of extending vocabulary and building new opportunities whilst trying to maintain familiarity.

Starting points:

- Write a list of the common routine activities and transitions for an AAC user.
- How can AAC be incorporated?
- What language could be modelled during these activities?
- How will you extend and enhance the routine with chances to progress language over time?

Transitions are a crucial part of a learner's day; again, try to avoid over helping learners. Allow them time to 'have a go', and if they need help, this is a good opportunity for them to request help through their AAC. For example supporting them to zip up their coat be sure to direct them to their AAC if they need help.

During the early stages of establishing intentional communication, learners could be offered preferred items against non-preferred ones. Build into activities offering items they do not like or do not need. Chunk all activities to build communication.

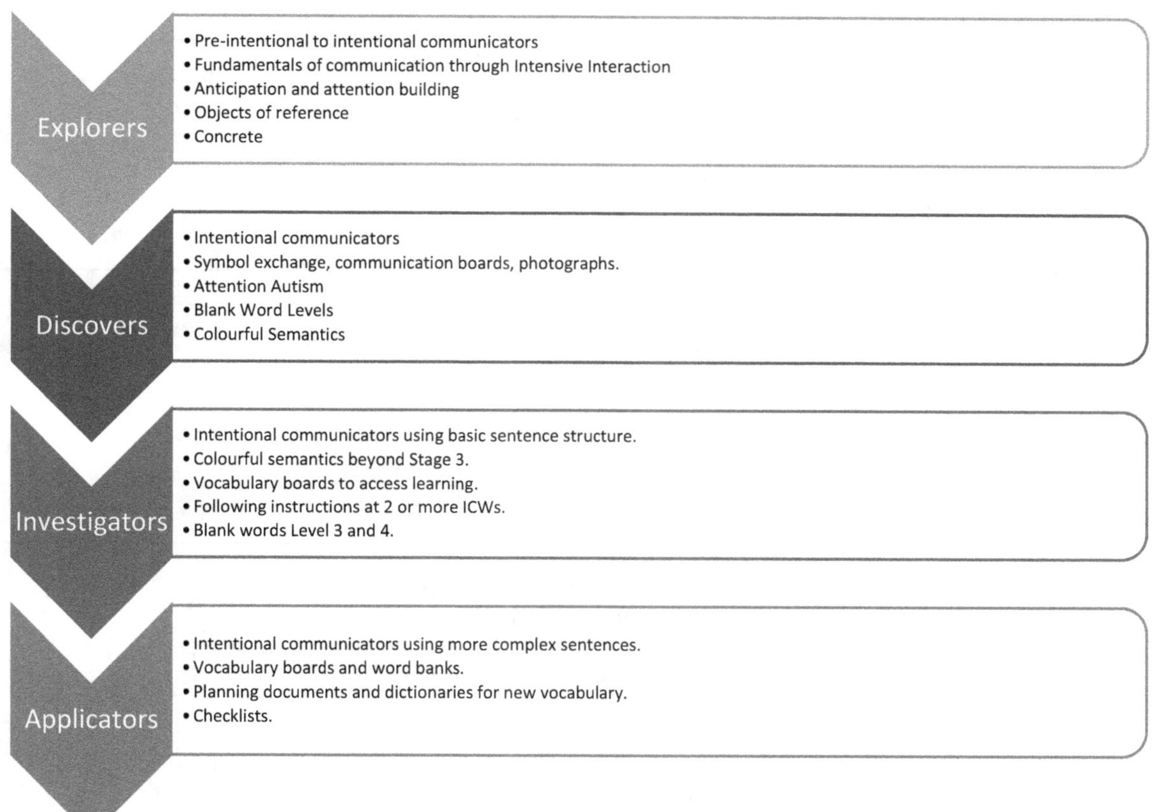

Figure 7.11 Total Communication Pathway

Step 8: The Connectivity Curriculum Requires a Total Communication Approach

Total Communication (Figure 7.11) is based on the idea that any means of communication is valuable. Embedding a variety of methods such as gestures, signs, drawing, writing, facial expression, body language, and symbols. There are extensive benefits to a Total Communication approach to ensure all modes of communication are not overlooked. Learners with complex needs, when struggling to communicate, can experience frustration and sometimes dysregulation. In some cases, the difficulties are so great that the young person 'gives up'. We can lessen frustrations by offering learners an alternative to just speech. Total Communication approaches help motivate and promote communication for all and will not hinder or replace the development of speech if this is achievable for the young person.

Step 9: Communication Checklist

As you progress with planning, it is always useful to pause and reflect on the learning you are implementing. Consider how your observations help you understand what a learner needs next.

Table 7.4 Communication Checklist

Fundamentals of Communication	1.	Pre-intentional communication
	2.	Anticipation of an event
	3.	Anticipation of an interaction
	4.	Consistent response
	5.	Development of joint attention
Intentional Communication	6.	Pointing
	7.	Initiation and Making Choices
	8.	Development in play skills from exploratory to imaginative. Supported turn-taking within play activities.
	9.	Understanding one information-carrying word. Responding to what and where questions.
	10.	Combining words/symbols/signs in short sentences. Understanding two information-carrying words. Responding to what, where, and how.
Verbal and Written Communication	11.	Combining words/symbols/signs in sentences. Understanding three information-carrying words. Responding to what, where, how, and why.
	12.	Able to include adjectives and additional information to extend sentences.
	13.	Able to use social skills to sustain an interaction. Play becoming collaborative. Able to speak or write with purpose.
	14.	Able to generalise communication skills in different settings and situations. Use functional communication skills to access local community and wider.

Step 10: Communication Progression Guidance and the Role of MKO

1. Pre-intentional Communication

At this stage, learners tend to respond to changes in their bodies or react to events instigated by adults or others around them. Vocalisations and body movements tend to relate to how comfortable they are feeling or discomfort. Adults supporting learners are responsible for interpreting these responses and acting accordingly. Changes in behaviour and sounds convey what the young person needs, likes or dislikes.

This communicative stage is similar to early infancy when a mother responds to the needs of her new baby.
Communication Partner Role

- *To interpret body movements, vocalisations, and facial expressions and assign meaning.*
- *Ensure you give a 'pause' to allow response time.*
- *To communicate meaning to their responses – preferences by stating '... you like this' or alternatively '... you don't like this.' Always use learners' names.*

- *To use repetitive routines to develop anticipation of events.*
- *Use people play regularly and broaden sensory experiences, encouraging active exploration.*

Anticipating Communication:

Over time, by following familiar routines, learners combine sensory information about an event and start to recognise what is going to happen. This anticipation of an event is communicated by a change in vocalisation, facial expression, or physiological response. The response from the learner happens just before the event.

This is an important milestone for both communication and cognitive development.
Communication Partner Role:

- *To acknowledge the anticipation of when it happens. Then look for the same response repeated next time, ideally becoming consistent to the same stimuli or event.*
- *Encourage vocalisation.*
- *Introduce objects of reference to link to daily activities.*
- *Use people play and intensive interaction to develop the fundamentals of communication.*

Interventions to promote engagement

- Intensive interaction
- People play – i.e. peek-a-boo; ready, steady, go; and rocking games.
- Objects of reference

2. *Building Focus and Joint Attention*

Joint attention is the shared focus on an object by two individuals and is achieved by one individual alerting another to the object by eye pointing, pointing or other verbal or non-verbal indications[5].

There are progressive steps to developing joint attention.

1. Mutual gaze – communicators give eye-to-eye contact.
2. Gaze following – communication partner can draw attention to specific objects.
3. Coordinated joint looks – this stage has three steps and is initiated by the young person. This can be to look at an object, person, then back to the object or person, object and back to the object.
    - Showing – this is when a learner will hold up an object to show to someone.

- Intentional following gaze – able to follow a gaze at a person or object consistently.
- Reaching and giving items.
- Following the point of another person.
- Pointing with clear communicative intent.

Joint attention needs to be established before a child can understand or start to point.
As the communication partner, you will need to consider:

- *Use the learner's name and hold objects in the learner's line of vision. Alternatively, respond to learners by picking up something in their eye line.*
- *Develop visual skills, including tracking skills.*
- *Encourage eye contact during interactions.*
- *Respond to the learner's gaze and give meaning to their eye pointing by giving them the object.*
- *Develop object permanence skills to support joint attention.*
- *Teach joint attention specifically using motivating objects of interest.*

3. *Intentional Communication: Initiation and Choices*

Through these stages, the learner can control and use body movements, posture, and vocalisation to send a purposeful message.

Learners can use vocalisations, movements, or verbalisation to initiate an increasing range of messages through their communication means.

- Requesting an object/action/information
- Answering
- Protesting
- Commenting

When a child can make clear choices, introduce changes to extend a child's communicative behaviour and thinking.
As the communication partner, you will need to consider:

- *Encourage the young person to imitate sounds, actions, and gestures.*
- *Encourage early requests in familiar, everyday routines to begin with, for example, snack time.*
- *Check if the learners can look at the same object and action as the supporting adult.*

- *Ensure as many opportunities as possible for learners to be able to communicate.*
- *Learners need to start communication using objects (most concrete). Cognitively learners need to be able to match photographs to objects, then symbol to photograph, to ensure the right means is used to support choice making.*

Interventions to encourage sharing experiences.

- When objects or other mediums are used in choosing to hold at eye level and label the item as they are presented, move the item slightly as you speak to draw attention to it. Repeat if necessary. Allow processing time.
- Introduce communication boards with core and fringe vocabulary to support access to learning activities.
- Build in choice-making into the majority of learning experiences.
- Introduce Attention Autism to increase learners' ability to attend.
- Introduce Colourful Semantics Stage 1.
- Plan learning activities to develop matching skills so pre-verbal learners can progress from objects to symbols.
- When a learner can make a clear choice between two items, then introduce changes; a third choice, sabotage through making a mistake, extend interests, or miss something out.
- Use visuals to communicate daily routines or task planners. Develop a clear start and finish to learning experiences.

Step 11: Progression in Play from Exploratory to Imaginative

We established the development of play is closely linked to the development of language.

Initially, a child will put everything in their mouth to explore items. Through mouthing, handling objects and observing others, learners begin to develop their own understanding of the purpose of an object. It is important that all learners have multi-sensory learning experiences. Modelling is key to enabling our learners to progress.

Exploring everyday objects, as well as toys, is important for learners to establish function, what it is made of, and what it is associated with supports learners to retain the word.

1. Imaginative play progresses in a developmental sequence.
   - Large doll/teddy play
   - Small world (miniature toys)
   - Play with pictures (puzzles/books)
   - Pretend play (dressing up and role play).

Through play experiences and adult support, learners will be supported in progressing from solitary play to parallel then onto social play.

As the communication partner, you will need to:

- *Provide opportunities to define objects, especially everyday items.*
- *Model how to use items and rehearse labelling.*
- *Use a turn-taking narrative, 'Jonny's turn, Laura's turn'.*
- *Provide learners opportunities to act out everyday routines using large dolls or soft toys.*
- *Use small world toys to support the curriculum theme.*
- *Observe the transfer and generalisation of the skills learned within the classroom.*
- *If at the pretend play stage, introduce a role-play corner within the classroom.*
- *Use rule-based play, e.g. Picture lotto, skittles, pop-up pirates, to develop social skills. Use a turn-taking board if it helps.*

2. Attention and Listening Skills

There can be a mismatch between learners' cognitive abilities and their attention skills. It is important to know at which stage of attending learners are, as this may be below integrated attention. Difficulties in attention can result in limited academic progress.

As the communication partner, you will need to consider:

- *Use the checklist to identify attention levels.*
- *Focus learners' attention by using their name. Use an appropriate level of language.*
- *Check if learners have understood where possible.*
- *Ensure learners are aware of their learning objectives.*
- *Introduce learning breaks to ensure learners are ready to learn.*
- *Do not expect learners to listen for too long, and ensure activities are varied.*
- *Teach learners how to listen – use visuals to support understanding.*
- *Consider where learners sit.*
- *Reduce background noise and distractions.*

Interventions to sustain attention

- Attention Autism
- Talking Boxes.

Learners who have attention and listening difficulties and require support to transfer and generalise communication skills.

How do Talking Boxes work?

- The activities can be used as single activities or a sequence.
- They can be used in a small group or with individual children.
- Each session should be between 5–10 minutes, depending on the age and interest of the children.
- If you use the activities in a group, then it is best to have 2 adults: one to lead the activities and one to support the children.
- Link the contents to the curriculum theme.

Step 12: Written Communication

Enabling learners to produce written, recorded (speech to text), symbols or print outcomes of their thoughts and ideas.

At this stage, learners need to be able to verbalise, sign, or combine symbols to produce sentences. Learners can verbalise or demonstrate using high-tech or low-tech communication systems.

To achieve the outcomes for this stage, learners must be able to:

1. Reach Level 4 of Blank Word Level Assessment.
2. Reach Stage 5 of Colourful Semantics.
3. Be able to express a sentence verbally, or via sign or symbol.
4. Ensure receptive language understanding is at two information-carrying words, showing retention of more complex instructions.
6. Use core and fringe vocabulary in a low-tech or high-tech communication aid.

Step 13: Implementing the Right Intervention

1. Intensive Interaction

Developed in the 1980s, Intensive Interaction is a social communication approach (see Table 7.4) that is most often used with people who have severe or profound and multiple learning difficulties and/or autism[6].

It teaches and develops the 'Fundamentals of Communication', attainments such as:

- enjoying being with others,
- sharing personal space,
- use and understanding of eye contact,
- facial expressions,
- using vocalisations meaningfully,
- taking turns in exchanges of conversation
- the structure of conversation.

Intent: To teach and develop interaction and communication through activities which are relaxed, pleasurable, and motivating for the learner. To advance learners from pre-intentional to intentional communicators to be able to progress onto communication systems.

What this looks like in the classroom

Intensive interaction often takes place between a learner and a supporting adult. The sessions can be timetabled but should also be spontaneous, with adults taking advantage of all possible opportunities to support positive interactions.

Implementation: Learners on the Explorer pathway will use Intensive Interaction as a primary means to learn about social interaction and establish the fundamentals of communication.

2. Attention Autism

Davies[7], the founder of Attention Autism, described the aims as developing natural and spontaneous communication through highly motivating visual activities. The programme builds up gradually, starting with one activity, and over time, increasing to four, supporting learners to gradually increase the amount of time they can attend and focus.

Stage one – involves the learners watching an adult explore or play with three items/toys that are hidden away in a container (normally a bucket).

Stage two – involves learners watching an adult complete a task. This can be an art/craft activity or a science-based activity.
Stage three – involves the learners watching an adult complete a fun task and then trying to complete it themselves.
Stage four – involves the learners watching the adult completing a tray-based work activity and then taking a tray and attempting to complete the work themselves.

Intent: To increase attention in learners during adult-led activities. To increase non-verbal and verbal communication through commenting. To build wealth and depth of vocabulary.

Implementation: This intervention is aimed at complex learners with fleeting attention.

3. Communication Book

A communication book is a folder with pages of symbols set out in topics and with core vocabulary on the back of each page. The folder is designed to help learners move between pages to link symbols with menu pages and tabs on the side of pages. It also contains a spelling page. Learners learn how to use the book through a 'Communication Partner' who models its use by pointing to the symbols while they talk to the learners. There are five stages with learners moving through them at their own pace. The core vocabulary is increased in each stage, as is the number of symbols on each topic page.

Intent: To teach and develop a functional means of communication which gives the learner a rich and varied vocabulary.

Implementation: All learners developing vocabulary and starting to combine symbols in their responses.

4. Makaton

Makaton is a unique language programme that uses symbols, signs, and speech to enable learners to communicate. It supports the development of essential communication skills such as attention and listening, comprehension, memory, recall, and organisation of language and expression.

Makaton uses speech with signs (gestures) and symbols (pictures) to help learners communicate. Facial expression, eye contact, and body language are also used to give as much information as possible.

Intent: To teach and develop the use of signs alongside speech to support learners with little or unclear speech.

Table 7.5 Intensive Interaction Progression

	Stage	Target
Intensive Interaction Targets	Stage 1	Learners will tolerate you joining in with their activities.
		Learners will tolerate you copying their sounds, actions, movements and emotions.
	Stage 2	Learners will appear to, fleetingly, notice you are there.
		Learners will pause from self-absorbed behaviour to fleetingly watch what you are doing.
		Learners will pause from self-absorbed behaviour to briefly watch what you are doing.
	Stage 3	Learners will begin to pay more consistent attention to you. They will pause and watch what you are doing more frequently.
		Learners will notice you are there and begin to respond.
		Learners will demonstrate any of the following: make eye contact, smile, show excitement, enjoyment, frustration, or satisfaction.
		Learners will begin to respond by continuing their actions/vocalisations and 'testing' or checking whether you copy them.
	Stage 4	Learners will be sustained in looking, listening or following events with movement of their eyes, head or other parts of their bodies.
		Learners will continue to engage in their own activity, but pay you more attention.
		Learners will show interest in what you are doing by giving constant attention.
	Stage 5	Learners will indicate they want more through either eye contact, facial expressions, touch, or vocalisation.
	Stage 6	Learners take responsibility for the continuation of the activity.
		Learners begin to lead more of the interaction.
		Learners communicate by their own means that they want to play or interact with you; maybe a game you have played before.
	Stage 7	Learners' interactions with you are less repetitive or self-absorbed. They independently start the interactions.
		Learners engage with you in an activity for social intent, e.g. they would rather do the activity with you than alone.
		Learners show you something they have been looking at.
		Learners will lead you to or indicate something they would like to share with you.

Implementation: All learners in school benefit from a total communication approach that incorporates Makaton. It is a socially engaging form of communication.

5. Voice Output Communication Aids (VOCAs)

VOCAs are specialised devices used for communication. They let learners 'speak' words and sentences electronically. They normally take the form of hand-held electronic devices that play words or phrases when the user touches a switch or presses buttons or keys. Some devices 'speak' words as the words are typed on a keyboard. Apps can be downloaded to tablets so that they can become speech-generated devices.

There are many different types, from single message outputs like switches to overlay models, GoTalks. The more specialist and complex VOCAs are eye gaze, tech talk, iPads with Proloquo2Go app, or grid apps. High-tech devices are usually supplied or recommended and provided by Speech and Language Therapists.

Table 7.6 Attention Autism Progression

Attention Autism Targets	Stage 1	Alerts to objects by body stilling Reactive response to stimuli Alerts to dominant stimulus presented by an adult Able to focus attention on a series of 3 objects presented from the Bucket, lasting 2 minutes in total Tolerates not handling objects from the bucket.
	Stage 2	Able to focus and sustain attention to 3 objects in bucket and one activity lasting 2 minutes Tolerates not handling objects demonstrated in the activity.
	Stage 3	Able to sustain attention to 3 objects in bucket and two structured activities led by an adult. Able to wait for their go Able to take a turn independently on adult's invitation Able to return to seat after taking turn independently and redirect attention to watching. Tolerates not always being able to have a turn.
	Stage 4	Able to watch adult complete simple task. Independently takes tray containing task to table. Attempts to complete the task while watching a supporting adult. Returns the tray to the leading adult.

Intent: To teach and develop a personalised method of functional communication. Ideally, learners should have access to their devices all the time. Learners should have individual sessions to develop skills. Devices should be incorporated into lessons. Implementation: International pre-verbal communicators or learners with Speech Disorders.

6. *Colourful Semantics*

Colourful semantics was designed by Bryan[8], and is a psycholinguistic approach that is often used to develop children's speech and writing abilities. It teaches children about the structure of a sentence by following the coloured coded order and categorisation of vocabulary.

Intent: Colourful semantics can help children develop their grammar, but the approach is rooted in semantics. Learners are taught to respond to key questions to support the development of sentence structure. An effective way of using colour to scaffold children's understanding of how words are linked in sentences.

- Extending from just keywords, making sentences longer.
- Supports sequencing words in the correct order.
- Development of grammar beyond key words (prepositions, pronouns, etc.).
- Vocabulary development.
- Understanding question words, e.g. Who? Where?

Table 7.7 Communication Book Progression

Communication Book Targets	Stage1	Learners show interest and awareness as communication partners use the book while they are chatting.
	Stage 2	Learners will point to single symbols during activities. Learners show interest as the communication partner extends the communication they have used (e.g. learner points to 'ball', communication partner points to 'want + ball') Learners show interest as the communication partner uses the spelling page. Learners begin to combine two symbols. Learners link a core symbol with a topic symbol.
	Stage 3	Learners will begin to link three to four ideas using symbols. Learners will begin to take responsibility for locating topic pages within the book. Learners will include descriptions when combining symbols. Learners show interest as the communication partner using the 'question' page. Learners will begin to use the spelling page after it has been modelled by the communication partner.
	Stage 4	Learners initiate using the communication book. Learners regularly combine three or more symbols. Learners will incorporate symbols from quick link pages into their symbol combinations. Learners will begin to question, negotiate, reason, and plan using the appropriate symbols. Learners will begin to clarify meaning using the intent and time symbols on the topic pages. Learners will use the spelling page in a structured activity.
	Stage 5	Learners will use the communication book to give and share information. Learners will use the communication book to describe situations and objects. Learners will use the communication book to exchange personal stories, thoughts, and opinions. Learners will use the communication book to gain information about the world. Learners will use the communication book to play and work with others. Learners will use the communication book to reason and predict. Learners will use the communication book to evaluate their performance. Learners will use the communication book to negotiate. Learners will use the communication book to make plans.

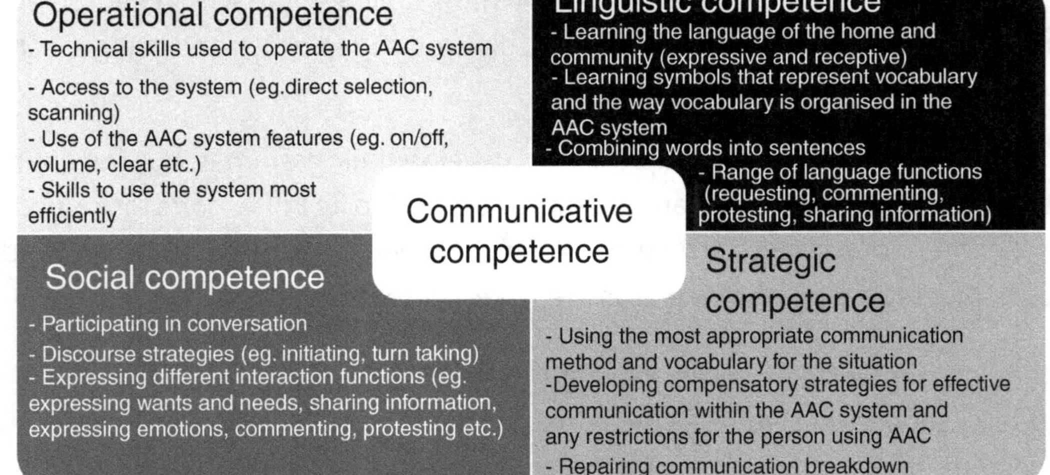

Figure 7.12 Setting Goals for Augmentative Alternative Communication. As cited in Kovach (2009) Augmentative & Alternative Communication Profile (AACP), LinguiSystems

Figure 7.13 Colourful Semantics. As cited in Ogg (2013) Colourful Semantics. The Practical Resource, STASS Publications Ltd.

Who = orange
What doing = yellow
What = green
Where = blue
When = brown
Adjectives = purple
Grammar = white square
How = pink

- Storytelling.
- Literacy.

Implementation: Supports progression from combining symbols/words to written output. Colorful Semantics can be used within subject specific learning as well be embedded within the environment. Targetting:

- Learners with receptive language difficulties.
- Learners with expressive language difficulties.
- Learners who have difficulties understanding and answering questions.
- Learners who omit words.
- Learners who lack variety in their sentence content.

7. The Blank Language Scheme (Blank Levels)

The blank language scheme or the language learning model was devised in 1978 (Blank et al. 1978)[9]. It encourages the development of children's verbal reasoning and abstract language. The model breaks the area of language into four steps/levels.

Level 1 = Naming
Level 2 = Describing
Level 3 = Re-telling
Level 4 = Justifying

Intent: To develop verbal reasoning skills.

Table 7.8 Colourful Semantics Progression

Colourful Semantics Targets		
	Stage 1	Introduce the 'who' orange cue card and environmental photos linked to learners and staff. Able to match one symbol to a familiar person. Progress to the subjects in pictures.
	Stage 2	Introduce 'who' and 'what doing' yellow cue card. Introduce verbs alongside activities within PE – running, jumping, and throwing. Learners can combine two symbols matched to a photograph or illustration. Subject + verb. Learners can match the symbols to a colour scaffold.
	Stage 3	Continue Stages 1 and 2. Introduce a third cue card, 'what', linked to the object. Learners can combine three symbols matched to a photograph or picture. Subject + verb + object. A matching scaffold can be used too to enable learners to organise their ideas.
	Stage 4	Continue Stages 1 to 3. Introduce a fourth cue card for 'where' linked to location. Learners can combine four symbols matched to a photograph or picture. Subject + verb + object + place. A matching scaffold can be used too to enable learners to organise their ideas.
	Stage 5	Continue with Stages 1 to 4. Introduce adjectives to describe a subject, object, or place. Learners can combine five symbols matched to a photograph or picture. Adjective + subject + verb + object + place. A matching scaffold can be used too to enable learners to organise their ideas. Subject + verb + adjective + object + place. Subject + verb + object + adjective + place.
	Stage 6	Continue with Stages 1 to 5. Introduce a 'when' cue card linked to time. Learners can combine five or six symbols to form an extended sentence. Time + subject + verb + object + place. Subject + verb + object + adjective + place + time.
	Stage 7	Introduce grammar and connectives to develop literacy skills. (These words are introduced on a white background.)
	Stage 8	There is an additional cue card for 'how' to develop complex sentences. This might be a stage that some learners find too abstract. Alternatively, learners can develop confidence by reducing the matching element within their writing. They can attempt to write a sentence and check the structure with a visual afterwards when reading it back.

Implementation: All learners will be asked the correct level of questions during lessons and in everyday situations.

Step 14: Progress Measures

It is important, as practitioners, to assess learning. The trackers provided for each intervention will enable you to identify not only the learner's starting point, but they will also enable the tracking of progress and identification of the small steps needed to achieve a stage. The trackers will support considered implementation of a sequential curriculum.

Table 7.9 Blank Word Level Progression

Blank Word Level	Level 1	Learners answer a 'What is this?' question. Learners respond to a 'Find me a ...' request. Learners respond to a 'Find me another one like this' request. Learners respond to a 'Where is the ...?' Learners respond to a 'Which one is the...?' question. Learners can say what they have heard. Learners can say what they have touched. Learners can say what they have seen. Learners can name an object in a simple picture or photograph.
	Level 2	Learners respond to a functional question, 'Which do we use to dig?' Learners complete a sentence, 'You water the garden with....' Learners understand things that go together: 'What goes with a fork?' Learners can respond to things about an object, 'Find me one that is big and red' Learners can sort or categorise and name differences when objects are in sight: 'What else can grow in the ground?' 'Name another plant'. Learners can name parts of an object, e.g. pen lid Learners understand linguistical concepts, 'Find a big pot, find a black pot, find two pots'. Learners can describe a scene, 'What is happening?' Learners can answer 'what, who, where' questions; remember simple information.
	Level 3	Learners can find an object by using verbal and visual information. Learners can describe what might happen next when given a sequence of pictures. Learners can say what they think a person might say or think. Learners can make general comments about something that's happened: 'What happened to all of these?' Learners can follow a set of directions, 'Do this and then this'. Learners can give a set of directions. Learners can arrange pictures in a sequence. Learners can tell a story from a set of pictures. Learners can summarise a story Learners can find and describe similarities, 'How are these the same'. Learners understand negatives, finding an item or a group that 'is not'. Learners can define words.
	Level 4	Learners can explain and justify a prediction. Learners can identify the cause of an event. Learners can think of and explain a solution. Learners can think of and explain a solution from someone else's point of view. Learners can explain how to reach a goal. Learners can explain why, 'Why would you use a pan?' Learners can explain why something cannot be done. Learners can explain, and an inference can be drawn from what they see: 'How can we tell?'

Summary

The successful implementation of a Connectivity Curriculum needs a good understanding of the starting points of your young people with complex learning needs. As practitioners, 'assessment for learning' is key and will allow for the necessary evaluation for when to move forward with fundamental skills. The interventions shared are reputable and evidence-based. The careful planning of combining the right interventions in a sequential manner will result in impactful achievement for all.

Notes

1 Wadham. A (2017) Cambridgeshire Therapeutic Thinking training materials. Course attended 16th October 2017.
2 Dix. P (2017) *When The Adult Changes Everything Changes*. Crown House.
3 Mahler. K (2019) The Interoception Curriculum: A Step-by-Step Guide to Developing Mindful Self-Regulation. www.kelly-mahler.com 26 July 2024.
4 Kuypers. L (2011) *The Zones of Regulation*. Publisher: Social Thinking.
5 Paparella. T, Stickles-Good. K, and Kasari. C (2011) The Emergence of Non-verbal Joint Attention and requesting Skills in Young Children with Autism. *Journal of Communication Disorders* Vol 44 pp 569–583.
6 Hewett. D (2012) *The Intensive Interaction Handbook*. SAGE Publications Ltd.
7 Davies. G (2023) Attention Autism: A Comprehensive Guide for Teachers. www.inclusiveteach.com 14 September 2023.
8 Bryans. A (1997) Colourful Semantics. www.integratedtreatmentservices.co.uk 29th July 2024.
9 Blank. M, Rose. S, and Berlin. L (1978) The language of learning: the preschool years. New York: Grune & Stratton.
10 Money. D, and Thurman. S (1994) Talkabout Communication. *Bull College Speech Lang Therap*. 504: pp 12–3.

8

Connectivity Curriculum: Impact

The youngest person I (Laura) have ever taught joined our area special school class at two and a half years of age. He was pre-verbal and had not yet developed full head control. To gain his attention through people play, we created a giant, human, jack-in-the-box – a very large box painted in bright colours, with orange drapes hanging over the top. Staff members took turns to be in the box. When a Big Mac switch was pressed, 'hello', up jumped a staff member calling out, 'hello'. Not only did we develop cause and effect, but we were also developing head control when he was positioned over a wedge.

We worked tirelessly on his sensory and physical development, and at the age of six, he took his first steps. We had progressed through numerous specialist chairs; initially providing full body support to gradually removing supports as we progressed to a regular classroom chair with arms. As physical strength increased, communication skills developed linearly through switches and communication boards.

This section explains how play is the main medium for gauging the impact of the Connectivity Curriculum. It offers three in-depth case studies of how a Connectivity Curriculum was introduced in different school settings: preschool, special school, and mainstream primary. The structure of the curriculum is mapped against the domains identified in S.P.I.C.E. (see Chapter 2, Figure 2.1). We hope that these examples can enhance your understanding of how our ideas relate to practice and can support you in adapting the approach to your own context.

Impact[1]

Play is the key medium for gauging the learning and functional communication of young people with complex needs. The right to play is treasured in the articles within the Rights of Every Child[2]. The fundamental role of play in promoting learning, and there needs to be planned opportunities, up to the age of seven, within the primary curriculum[3].

DOI: 10.4324/9781003301004-8

The government publications for Special Education Needs, Commission on Assessment Without Levels[4] and The Rochford Review[5] promote alternative assessment styles which have the young person's individuality at the centre.

McIntosh promoted schools measuring all aspects of progress, including communication, social skills, physical development, resilience and independence. This was reinforced by Rochford when her review outcomes stated that assessment arrangements should work for all pupils, whatever their needs or circumstances. Sheridan[6] states communication is a complex process, and it is important for young people to have every opportunity to rehearse and transfer their learning, and play appears to be the ideal medium. The Royal College of Speech and Language Therapists[7] produced a document outlining five standards for making reasonable adjustments to ensure people with learning disabilities and/or autism communication are prioritised when meeting their needs to support them to lead fulfilling lives within their communities. The document supports the idea of young people with severe learning difficulties being lifelong learners, a key principle of the Connectivity Curriculum. From an education perspective, there needs to be a starting point. MacIntyre[8] expresses that the focus should come from their maturational stage and natural desires to encourage development. He continues with learning opportunities that need to begin with where the child is, then begin to build in small steps. Finally, MacIntyre summarises that the only way to know if a child has learnt something is to observe carefully and note any changes in what they do or what they communicate, which can be achieved when observing play.

Recording learning and development can be supported by the Engagement Model for learners starting at the Explorer Pathway. Carpenter[9] explains the importance of attention and engagement as the predictor of successful learning outcomes and meaningful learning. The Engagement Profile puts the child at the centre of assessment and recording. Carpenter acknowledges that hard-to-reach learners have an interest that will capture their attention. This discovery can then be transferred to practice in the classroom to increase learning impact. The indicators of the Engagement Profile are exploration, initiation, anticipation, persistence, and realisation.

Exploration: As an observer, you are assessing how interested and curious a learner is in a stimulus or an activity. Exploration becomes more established when the learner is still responsive to the same stimuli or activity when it is presented in a different context or environment. Exploration is important when gauging what motivates a learner and holds their attention to encourage further investigation and development of new knowledge and skills.

Realisation: As an observer, you are looking for learners to interact with a familiar stimulus or activity with the intent to discover new aspects or make changes. The application of new skills and knowledge is a key element of realisation.

Anticipation: As an observer, you are looking for the learner to be able to predict, expect or associate an outcome from a stimulus or activity. Being able to engage from the start to the finish of a learning experience. Anticipation aids a learner's memory and sequencing abilities.

Persistence: As an observer, you are assessing how the learner sustains their engagement with a stimulus or a learning activity, enabling them to take on new learning. Persistence is important because once established, a learner can develop, reinforce, and apply their skills and knowledge in various contexts.

Initiation: A learner can demonstrate the different ways they can investigate within their learning to bring about different outcomes. The learner will act independently and spontaneously within a familiar activity. Initiation is key to developing independence.

The aim is to study and observe young people with complex learning needs to know their Engagement Profile because knowing what they are most interested in can then be embedded within their learning activity, and elements that excite them are more likely to lead to realisation. The Engagement Model is made up of three interdependent parts. Stage 1 is the profile; how does the young person look when they are engaged? Profiling provides a representation of the young person's voice and is an important step to developing personalised learning.

From the profile, practitioners then monitor engagement, assessing content and strategies to optimise engagement. Thinking of the profile as the young person's pedagogy, schema, you are looking to grow and generalise them so learning occurs regularly throughout their day, week, and term. Finally, reflect on the Connectivity Curriculum, ensuring the content is meaningful to the young person with complex learning needs. Practitioners should always be looking to ensure learners are active participants. The evidence from the Engagement Model will validate the curriculum implementation strategies by maintaining or increasing engagement.

Case Study One

Early Intervention: Autistic With Profound Learning Difficulties (Complex Dual Diagnosis)

Sidney is the elder of the two brothers. He lives with both parents in their family home. Both parents are graduates and were at the start of their professional careers. Sidney was diagnosed with autism and with profound learning difficulties at three years of age, and he was referred to the Early Years Support Pathway that was part of the Local Offer for the county he lived in. Through the pathway, this gave him access to health professionals and SEND Services for early intervention.

Initial observations and anecdotal notes by health professionals, Community Paediatrician, and Speech and Language Therapist:

Parental concerns were from very early on (10 months) regarding unusual play and lack of communication. Repetative spinning wheels on cars or stroking his toy rabbit in an unusual way for long periods of time. Unusual mannerisms, such as body stiffening when tired. Parents described him as hard to reach/engage. Despite repatition he had pushed cars along and had recently thrown a ball. He had a toy washing machine, which he would put clothes in. Parents expressed that he would play with a toy very intensely but then lose interest. He used to like looking at books, but has lost interest. His favourite place is being outside and bouncing on the trampoline. He likes 'rough and tumble' play, especially tickling. Engagement is on his terms. He likes music and responds to music. Mum uses music to calm him down; she plays the same songs through his headphones. He is not really interested in TV but would watch Peppa Pig for a short time. His attention span is fletting.

Development: Walked around 12 months but didn't crawl. Not toilet-trained and had no awareness of this sensation (interoception). Sidney had a poor sleep pattern and frequently woke between midnight and 3.00 am. He can be awake for hours. Parents had tried Melatonin, but this wasn't helpful.

Receptive Understanding: Parents feel Sidney can understand some instructions, but these are on his terms and often ignored. Eye contact is minimal. Better with parents, but rarely makes eye contact with others. He ignores people most of the time.

Initiation: Food preferences are bacon and cake. Sidney would moan/cry when he was upset or wanted something (high-pitched cry) but does not always direct his communication to the adult. He would go and stand by mum or dad when he wants something but didn't communicate directly. Didn't point/lead. Intentional communication was limited.

Expressive Language: Historically, Sidney had said words in the past but not used them again and not used them communicatively. Didn't babble. Parents described baby brother's development as very different (he is babbling and is starting to say words; they felt his development was ahead of Sidney's in terms of communication and understanding. Occasionally Sidney would shake for no. He laughs to show pleasure, but does not direct/share pleasure often and sometimes laugh for no apparent reason.

Diet: Restricted range of foods and will not try new foods. Fishfingers for breakfast, sandwiches for lunch, and pasta for tea. Some yoghurt and a bit of cheese. Drank from a sippy cup.

Sidney was due to start pre-school that September. Parents were concerned about how he would manage, as he had no communication. Sidney did not get upset when separating from his parents.

Family Factors: The parent felt there was undiagnosed Autism on her side of the family; her grandmother had commented that Sidney was like her brother. Her brother was an academic and, although employed, was socially isolated and did not have relationships; her father presented similarly. Mother left school at 14 as she was unable to cope with the structure, self-educated until she went to university where she got a degree. Father is a research chemist and has a PHD in philosophy.

The Approaches Tried by Parents

- Reduced language to one keyword when giving instructions.
- Stage 1: symbol exchange, but Sidney was not ready for this communication system.
- Objects of reference initially. Then Sidney was introduced to a visual timetable using photographs.
- Intensive interaction alongside his play, for example, jumping with him.
- Parents attended workshops, *The Importance of Visuals and Early Language*, delivered by Speech and Language Therapists.

The Early Intervention Plan

- Sidney and his parents were welcomed into a peer group and introduced to other families and professionals.
- Sidney was encouraged to participate in play and learning activities appropriate to his level of need and development.
- Professionals modelled supportive strategies for Sidney's mother to familiarise with during play activities with a view to then generalise by using them at home.
- Practitioners modelled the use of visual support to help Sidney and his parents understand and implement the group routines at home.
- To provide an environment that encouraged Sidney to play alongside other children with a range of resources.

Creating an Enabling Environment

- The learning space was clearly defined with consistent spaces. A table for snacks, sensory play outside (sand and water), a floor-based play area with instruments, large blocks, wooden sensory exploration toys and shredded paper in the tuft tray. There was a table for posting and mark-making.
- Established a set routine. There was a visual schedule on A5-size cards, visible in the centre of the room. Play – hello – story circle – attention building – calm routine – snack – goodbye song. The free exploration/play section of the session lasted about 45 minutes before some items were covered with sheets or put away, ready for attention-building activities.
- Motivational and sensorimotor activities. Sand and water, as well as sensory toys that spin.
- Communication and social. Stop/go focus during play. Turn-taking dialogue: 'My turn, Sidney's turn.' Joint attention activities. Intensive Interaction during exploration/ sensory play. Choices between two objects at snack time.

Initially, Sidney was a passive observer within the group setting. Keeping his distance from others and soothing himself by stroking his soft rabbit toy repeatedly. Over time, intervention was introduced gradually.

SPICE Application (see Figure 8.1)

1. **Communication: On-body Signing.** We were able to teach 'stop/go' using on-body signing linked to Sidney spinning wheels during play. Sidney was unable to register

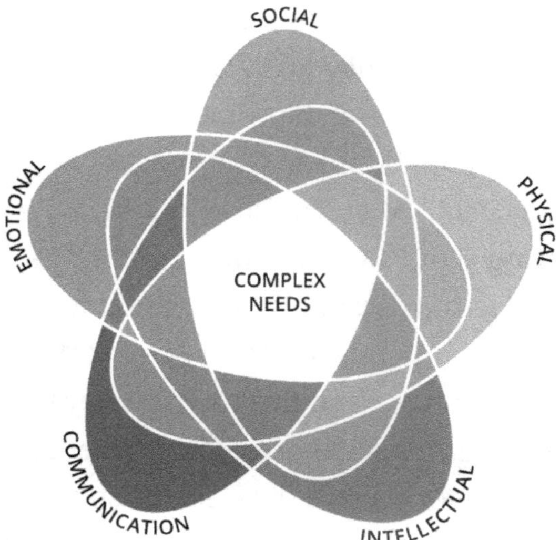

Figure 8.1 SPICE Model

communicative signals from supporting adults through words or gestures. When we paused the spinning of the wheel and offered him more. To ensure he registered the communication, we used on-body signals. Stop was taught through a hand on his chest when the wheel was stopped. When Sidney responded with a look at the wheel or a reach out, the communication partner would say 'go' and spin the wheel again. After several sessions, this developed to introducing 'more' in the pause. The communication partner would place their hands under Sidney's and bring them together, physically teaching him how to sign more. At week 7, his parent shared a video of this transferring to a swing at home and again using the on-body 'stop' and pause. Sidney independently signed more to request another push. Within the sessions, this was transferred to sand and water play.

2. **Intellectual: Readiness to Learn**. Sidney appeared to have low arousal levels and sought vestibular input to alert himself. A gym ball was introduced, and when Sidney was expected to engage in a cognition activity (an inset puzzle/mark making/shape sorter), he needed to be alerted. Bouncing on a gym ball enabled Sidney to be ready to learn. Once Sidney smiled and gave fleeting eye contact, he was directed to the table. Backward chaining was applied, for example, when an inset puzzle was introduced; all pieces were modelled, and Sidney put in the last piece. Within two sessions, Sidney was completing an inset puzzle with sound output when the first piece was modelled. Short burst activities were chunked by first bounce, then puzzle. Over the course of the sessions, Sidney accessed inset puzzles, shape sorters and made lines with cars for mark making.
3. **Social: Joint Attention and Turn-taking**. Sidney was assisted to sit during the attention-building activities. If he got up to walk away, he was directed back gently

for 'sitting'. Sidney was motivated by the slinky on the tactile story ring as this was shared around the group. Sidney was also engaged by bubbles. Sidney was encouraged to look towards the adult blowing the bubbles. Anticipation was built by using a consistent cue, '1,2,3 bubbles'. During tasks and free play, a turn-taking narrative was repeatedly used: 'My turn, Sidney's turn'.

4. **Emotional: Calm routine (TACPAC principles).** Sidney liked the tactile input from the objects used within the consistent routine. He sat for the longest periods during this calming activity. The routine built up from two short snippets of songs to three full songs. One action/object was used per song. Sidney would show preferences by moving to enable his mother to knead or brush different parts of his body. The final song was swaying back and forth whilst he held his soft rabbit. This was so effective for Sidney that his parents created a kit and had the song playlist on their phones. They would use it when out shopping or at new locations. A transferable regulation toolkit.
5. **Physical and Sensory**. Sidney needed access to physical activities such as bouncing and climbing. The gym ball was used throughout his session, and a small climbing frame was introduced to the outside area to ensure the sensory outlets Sidney required were readily available. The vestibular sensory tools reduced the amount of time Sidney would repeatedly travel up and down the picket fencing of the outside area, enabling him to engage in a wider variety of play activities within his environment.

Summary

The strategies modelled and developed enabled all adults supporting Sidney to be consistent in their delivery. Sidney responded positively to the calm routine, on-body signing, and vestibular alerting activities such as bouncing on the gym ball. The bouncing helped Sidney to be 'ready to....'. He also responded positively to anticipation and joint attention activities, demonstrating copying of actions and progression in play skills. He developed a greater awareness of those around him and engaged in group activities alongside his peers with adult support. Sidney waved goodbye once at the end of a session for the first time. His routines were implemented at the nursery and home, ensuring his early intervention was daily in all environments.

Reader Reflection

Have you met with parents to discover motivational activities?

Give yourself time to observe and assess the best means of communication.

Reflect on sensory processing and if the young person is hypersensitive or hypo sensitive to stimulation. Are they at an arousal level that enables them to engage?

Case Study Two

Special School Class: Cohort With Severe Learning Difficulties

All learners were between the ages of five to eight, and they all had complex communication needs and varying medical diagnoses, a neurodiverse class.

Ted: Cerebral Palsy, Global Developmental Delay, Severe/Profound sensorineural hearing loss, visual impairment and compensated Hydrocephalus. Preverbal good use of vocalisations and gesture combined with hand-under-hand signing.

Tom: Down Syndrome, Ventricular Septal Defect, Global Developmental Delay, Visual Impairment including Nystagmus, Bilateral Hearing Impairment, Hypermobility and an underactive Thyroid. Limited speech, good use of functional language, this, that, there, and mine, combined with signing and a communication book.

Lottie: Early Infantile Epileptic Encephalopathy (drug-resistant epilepsy), which required hemispherectomy surgery to remove and disconnect the right side of her brain. Following the surgery, LC-D has loss of movement and sensation to her left side. She has been seizure-free since the operation. Limited speech combined with adapted Makaton signs and a communication book.

Belle: Cerebral Atrophy with Hydrocephalus, Global Developmental Delay, and she is totally deaf in her right ear and wears a hearing aid to improve her hearing in the left ear. Non-verbal, good use of vocalisations and gestures combined with on-body signs and the symbol exchange communication system.

Sam: Down Syndrome, Global Developmental Delay, moderate bilateral sensory neural hearing loss and hypermobility, which affects his motor skills. Limited speech and basic Makaton signing.

Ollie: Quadriplegia, Cerebral Palsy, left femoral-head displacement, and cortical visual impairment. Non-verbal and expresses himself using a high-tech communication aid, the Accent 800.

Millie: Down Syndrome and Global Developmental Delay. Limited speech and limited signing.

Lewis: Down Syndrome, Global Developmental Delay and is currently being reviewed for Attention Deficit Hyperactivity Disorder and Reactive Attachment Disorder. Picture exchange communication system and limited speech.

Molly: Complex Epilepsy and Global Developmental Delay. Speech is good, but struggles to retain and sequence information.

Toby: Complex Epilepsy, Global developmental Delay and central vision loss. Basic speech struggles to retain information and lacks confidence.

The common denominator for all the young people in the class was that they have a diagnosis of Global Developmental Delay. Two of the children did have speech but had challenges in retaining information to relay their messages. Poor working memories impacted all the learners except one. The children required visual scaffolding and concrete learning materials, creating a multi-sensory pedagogy. The teaching of all the children required collaborative work from a multi-disciplinary team of health professionals to ensure the pedagogy met the needs of all.

The children were following a discovery pathway to support learning for life. The curriculum was topic-based with a structured timetable. They started every day with literacy, followed by movement maths. The afternoon sessions were topic-related and linked to Knowledge and Understanding the World and Expressive Arts. The main targeted interventions were Cued Articulation to support speech mechanics, Colourful Semantics activities linked to the class story and finally the See and Learn reading programme. The children were using Makaton signing and a dynamic communication book to scaffold their communication, following the repeated process 'make, read, sign/say'.

Creating an Enabling Environment

The room was transformed into an Early Years setting, having dedicated areas for:

- Reading
- Circle time
- Numeracy table
- Role play
- Small world
- Outside provision
- Craft area
- Sensory exploration

The children who were allocated laptops had a dedicated area for their technical equipment to ensure regular access to assistive technology.

The SPICE environmental checklist was applied. For the safe space, there was a corner of the room dedicated to soft furnishings, both on the floor and lower walls.

Table 8.1 S.P.I.C.E Environmental Checklist

	Think S.P.I.C.E Environmental Checklist
Emotional	Visual Timetable Safe space – soft cushions and a blanket Zones of Regulation – supports emotional check-ins. Regulation toolkits / Worry box or monster
Communication	Communication systems (AAC) Photographs of learners were displayed to remind them of experiences. Shared language – Be safe, be ready, and be kind. Welcome information – learner passports / engagement profile.
Intellectual	All draws to be labelled with symbols / photographs of resources. Working walls – key vocabulary / concepts / learning progression. Reading corner Scaffolds to promote independence – task planner, colourful semantics grid, sentence starters.
Physical	Physical boundaries of the classroom – defined areas Seating plan (photographs on chairs within circle) Lining up plan. Sensory Circuits / outside play equipment Mirrors to rehearse body awareness and articulation skills.
Social	Snack and breakfast table Alternative learning spaces – role play, small world, curiosity table. Sensory play/exploration area Class registration board – ten frames.

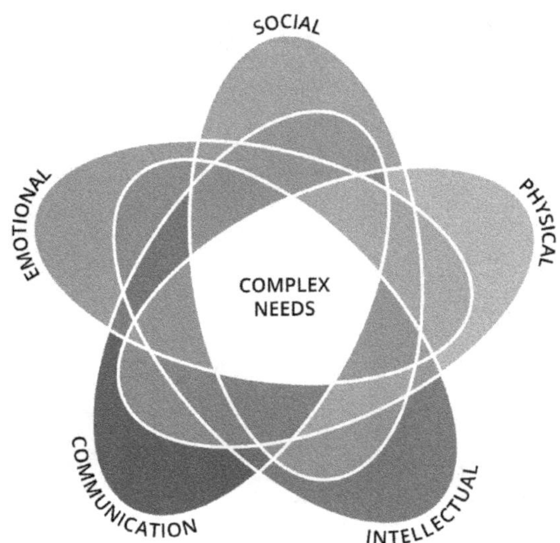

Figure 8.2 SPICE Model

SPICE Application (see Figure 8.2)

1. **Emotional: Relationships.** The relationships between the staff and the children needed to grow. The relationships between peers needed facilitation. Play was decided as the best medium to develop trusted relationships. Time was dedicated at the end of every day for child-led play. Role play was the most popular for the children, demonstrating their desire to act out scenarios including familiar characters or professionals. Hospital role play, doctors and nurses, was the most popular.

   Every learning session ended with a turn-taking game to build incentive and motivation. The type of games included Pig Goes Pop, Barbeque Party, Pop up Pirates, Hungry Hippos, Greedy Granny, Splashy Whale, Funny Face and Phil the Fridge. The one factor the games all shared was the build-up of anticipation before a surprise response was triggered. All the children were intrigued and excited to participate in the turn-taking games. The games not only supported social and emotional development but also internal impulse controls.

2. **Physical and Sensory: Sensory Strategies.** Sensory motor development was a priority area because some learning barriers and behavioural challenges derived from the children being unable to process and make sense of the sensory information messages coming from the world around them and their internal systems (interoception). Typically, developing children advance their sensory motor skills through physical play. Sensory circuits were set up daily, so the equipment was readily available throughout the day. It was also used daily as the 'ready to learn' transitional activity as the young people arrived at school.

Most of the children presented with sensory processing needs as outlined in Table 8.2.

3. **Communication: Total Communication Approach.** Combined communication techniques were used: Makaton signing, a communication book with dynamic symbols (make, read, sign/say), Cued Articulation, and Colourful Semantics. These systems were embedded in every activity. Vocabulary boards and cards accompanied learning through play.
4. **Intellectual: Consistent Routines.** Every morning, there was a consistent greeting circle time (familiar song and seating plan); the daily schedule was referred to, so the children knew visually what was expected of them and when. One child had an individual visual schedule for the day, and another a 'Now and Next' card. Two

Table 8.2 Sensory Profiles

		Behaviours observed	
Children	*Sensory system*	*Highly Sensitive*	*Low Sensitivity*
5 learners	Vestibular System (balance)	A poor sense of balance Unwillingness to leave the ground or take risks.	Unable to stay still – always on the go Difficulties sitting still Constant fidgeting and flapping Fast movements, but not always coordinated.
7 learners	Proprioceptive System (spatial awareness)	Removes self from busy places.	Stands close to others or pulls others in. Puts self into small places Bumping into things
3 learners	Visual System	Rubbing eyes and partially closing them.	
5 learners	Auditory System	Easily startled Easily distracted Likes to chew to damp down noises. Hesitation and longer delay in responding.	One student enjoys loud sounds.
5 learners	Tactile System	Fussy in regard to what they touch. Dislikes being touched; one student is particularly defensive about his head being touched. Loves hugs Dislike for messy play (avoids wet sensation with hands), and oppositely, several children really like messy play.	Heavy handedness Over-gripping Gets too close to others

The only system for which it was difficult to see, or no obvious behaviours were observed, was the olfactory system (taste and smell).

children followed an object of reference schedule. A targeted daily language and literacy session followed the morning circle time, incorporating Cued Articulation, See and Learn and Colourful Semantics. Attention-building activities were key components and delivered in the form of sensory stories, number and action songs, dough disco and Attention Autism.

Most children were effective at using a colour-coded scaffold to enable them to create a sentence when using Colourful Semantics resources, which was easily tailored to complement the language level the children were functioning at (one information-carrying word up to three), but more importantly, the visual scaffolding promoted combining words/symbols. To ensure connection in the curriculum the verbs (yellow) used in the Colourful Semantics related to the scenario text from See and Learn Phrases, focusing on everyday scenarios (brushing, eating, drinking, sleeping etc).

- The yellow cue card could be used to highlight the 'doing'words. Symbol-written learning objectives were quickly adapted to visualise what the expectation was by drawing focus to the verb in yellow symbols in the sentence. Schedules were adapted to include blue symbol cards to cue the children into when they were transitioning to a different location.
- For every sensory story, topic-based activity and exploratory learning, word banks were created to support the children accessing language visually and to experiment with joining the words together again following the Colourful Semantics.
- The visual scaffolding of a four-part sentence sequence was implemented into their conversation diary to encourage them to create a longer sentence and rehearse reading it back (make, read, say/sign).
- All the resources could easily be recreated on Clicker 7, following the same colour coded scaffold to create connectivity.

  Emphasis on the mouth (Cued Articulation theory) was strategically added over the Aurasma video modelling of the See and Learn everyday self-help scenarios. Again, the colour coding border was applied to verbs and objects within the videos. Combining interventions and integrating the principles across the classroom practice promotes connectivity. A connected multi-sensory approach developed around the young person and their everyday routines. The hypothesis is that communication and literacy skills would be enhanced due to the connectivity of the interventions delivered.

- Resources designed for multi-sensory delivery.
- Resources designed to 'free up thinking space' by providing a visual scaffold of language.
- A functional symbol system which can be understood by all audiences. A modelled system to encourage two-way communication.
- Motivation to communicate, especially through technology (microphones, iPads, and Apple TV).
- Motor planning, operation, and navigation are considered throughout, fixed-location keys, fringe folder system and readily accessible core vocabulary linked to every page.
- All elements of communication incorporated: requesting, naming, commenting, expressing, answering, and protesting.
- Development of a life skills profile for every student, which includes literacy skills (speaking, listening, reading, and writing).
- Differentiated and accessible resources for all SLD learners; Autistic Learners, Down Syndrome, and Global Developmental Delay.
- Independence and self-management are always promoted through video modelling and interactive schedules, which visualise the learning expectation.
- The process promotes consolidation, transferring, and generalisation of skills.

5. **Social: Independence.** There was a high dependency of the children on continuous adult guidance and reassurance. The SEN Code of Practice (2015)[10] promotes young people with SEN to maximise their independent potential and learning self-help skills. To address this ongoing concern, a practical work system was introduced. The pupils had to follow a visual sequence which required them to match the number to the corresponding tray, carry the tray to the table and sit independently to complete the activity. When they had completed their task and all were in the finished box, they checked it with a staff member. Three principles were applied to their visual system and tasks. Visual instruction (what is expected of them), visual organisation (aiding them in completing the task by modulating sensory input), and visual clarity (using colour coding or labelling to provide the important information) are all principles that support executive function. The system enables children to work alongside peers independently. The independence promoted in the system allowed every child an opportunity to build their confidence in their own abilities.

Summary

Through using the medium of play combined with a predictable routine, there was a noticeable reduction in difficult behaviours and an increase in parallel play within specific areas of the classroom. There was increased cooperation within play that was observed and then translated into learning activities. For example, the children worked as a team to make smoothies, sharing out resources and supporting each other through the process; when one pupil tried to cut the banana with the skin on, a peer voiced, 'peel it'. She then independently peeled the banana to slice.

Validation of the connectivity model within the classroom was provided by the school's Speech and Language Therapist. The initial language assessments were repeated, and eight students had progressed up a developmental stage in their communication skills. One student had progressed by two stages, and one student had remained within the same stage.

Feedback from the Speech and Language Therapist

Excellent attention and engagement throughout.

Trying hard to copy signs and spoken words +++.

Found named verb pictures 3/4 (did not know 'crying'). Using the Colourful Semantics sentence strip to prompt spoken/signed SV sentences. Added a word to this – 'boy kicking ball' – using spoken words and signs. Appeared to want to repeat sentences to make sure they were right.

Lots of subject-verb phrases were used during the session – copied and spontaneous.

Requesting – 'more bubbles' – following one adult model used spontaneously. Copied '__ _ on' when playing with Mr Potato Head.

Parents Evening Comments

'We are so pleased he is coming home and playing more with his sisters'.
'She is role playing school and describing how she is learning'.
'He is talking much more'.
'She wants to read all the time'.
'When we say the staff names, he gets excited'.
'He is turn taking and playing with figurines more'.
'We love the fact she can learn through play, because she is learning but not realising and she doesn't feel pressurised to learn'.

Reader Reflection

Have you addressed the sensory processing needs of individuals first?

Is your routine repetitive?

Do pupils feel safe and secure in their trusted relationships to allow them to be ready to learn?

A calm and relaxed environment where self-expression was celebrated. Play principles reduced academic pressure and lowered anxieties within young people, enabling supporting staff to discover how the children naturally learnt (schematic play).

Independence and self-efficacy (belief in their own abilities) are key for children with complex SEND needs to be lifelong learners.

Case Study Three

Mainstream Setting: Complex Social, Emotional and Mental Health (SEMH) needs.

Harry was eight years of age, finding it hard to attend in the mainstream classroom. He was at the expected age in his learning, with a strength in mathematics. He found English challenging, and writing was a barrier for him. A blank page made him feel overwhelmed. At times, he would subconsciously enter 'fight, flight or freeze' response when overwhelmed, especially if there was attention on him within the classroom. At transition points in the day, this would result in a 'freeze' response, and he would not be able to move from the spot he had planted, despite peers transitioning around him. Academic demand too soon afterwards resulted in a flooding of emotions and a 'flight' response; he would run and climb fences, or he would enter a different space, the school hall or library, and throw items or push furniture over. On one occasion, he hit out at the supporting staff member.

Harry had experienced Adverse Childhood Experiences (ACEs); his parents separated in his early life after and there was reported historical domestic abuse. Harry's mother had ongoing difficulties with her mental health. He moved from the custody of his mother to permanent custody of his father when he was seven years old. He had since had inconsistent contact with his mother. Harry's needs were classed as Social, Emotional and Mental Health.

The frequency of Harry's dysregulation was increasing, so a different approach was needed to reduce his anxiety and enable Harry to focus on his self-awareness and self-management. The long-term aim was always for him to reintegrate back into the mainstream classroom.

Assessments were conducted to provide a baseline measure. The online Boxall Profile was used in combination with a Strengths and Difficulties Questionnaire (SDQ).

Enabling Environment

A Nurture class was created to provide a comfortable and safe environment for Harry to access alongside nine peers with similar needs.

The room was designed to give a homely feel rather than a formal classroom. A sofa to provide a comfy, relaxing space, accompanied by a rug. It was important that there was a second, separate space in case pupils needed some time for themselves. There was a kitchen area to support daily breakfast, snacks, and a weekly cookery session. A sensory area with a floor mat and a large bean bag for a child who needed to jump and crash regularly to meet his proprioceptive needs.

There was a clearly defined workspace, which was set up as three workstations. This area was separated from the homely areas to develop the association of learning and maintaining expectations. A display board to showcase their work and progression; this

Table 8.3 Initial SDQ Outcomes

	Teacher		*Parent*	
Combined Scores	*Score*	*Outcome*	*Score*	*Outcome*
Emotional Problems Scale	10	Very High	7	Very High
Conduct Problems Scale	2	Close to Average	5	High
Hyperactivity Scale	10	Very High	8	High
Peer Problems Scale	5	High	2	Close to Average
Pro-Social Scale	6	Close to Average	9	Close to Average
Externalising Score	12	Very High	13	Very High
Internalising Score	15	Very High	9	High
Total Difficulty Score	27	Very High	22	Very High
Impact Score	3	Very High	4	Very High

allowed for reflection and celebration. Finally, a group table for structured play (Lego Therapy) and small group activities.

SPICE Application (see Figure 8.3)

1. **Communication: Pupil Voice.** The Functional Behaviour Assessment cards were used to gather Harry's' voice. Harry identified his strengths as computing and mathematics. He shared that he sometimes felt angry, especially when outside at break times. He shared that if he got angry, it would spoil his day. Harry said he knows he does not ask for help, he just worries.
   When accessing the association cards, Harry connected with the monster because he did not like how it felt when his body lost control. Harry then used cards to sort out what he was communicating when he became overwhelmed.

   - I find it hard to concentrate.
   - I feel out of control.
   - I do not want to cry in front of others.

   The final set of cards was his ideas of what might be helpful.

   - Using a time-out card (he shared he struggled to speak in front of others, so a card would help)
   - Having a safe space to go to.
   - The way people talk, he preferred a calm voice.
   - Less noise

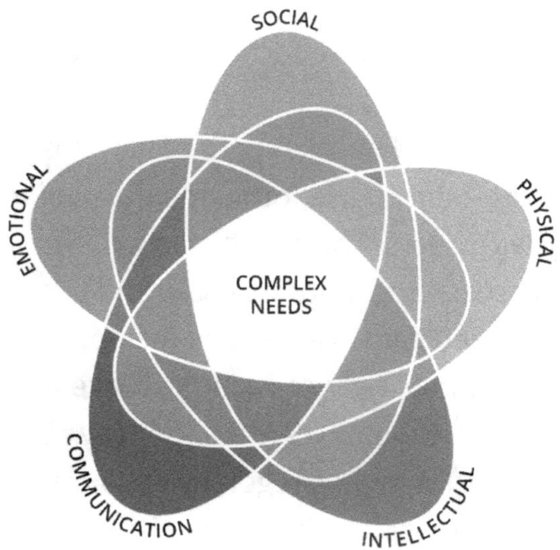

Figure 8.3 SPICE Model

- Having a break
- Harry's voice was included in the planning of his strategies to ensure all staff were consistent in meeting his needs.

2. **Emotional: Zones of Regulation.** Harry's negative feelings were fueling his difficult behaviours. He had regular feelings of being unsafe, loss, lack of trust, scared, angry, frustrated, disappointed, low self-worth, a sense of failure, and anxiety. The aim of the nurture class was to enable him to feel safe and secure, trusted, and valued, affirming a sense of belonging. Every morning, as part of his breakfast, he worked on using visuals from Zones of Regulation. Through the visuals, staff could interpret and support Harry to identify how he was feeling and which Zone this might relate to. If he was not yet in the green zone, a conversation was had about what he needed to enable him to get 'ready to learn' and reach the green zone. This could differ from a sensory break with a five-minute timer or a short Lego challenge. These strategies were added to his personalised toolkit that helped him to self-manage.
3. **Physical: Regulation.** Harry quickly discovered that physical activity helped him to remain regulated and manage his big emotions. The physical activities varied from kicking a ball with a peer, skipping or flipping tyres. The physical strategies for regulation soon became part of Harry's individualised toolkit.
4. **Intellectual: Assistive Technology.** Harry was able to access the mainstream curriculum at a slower pace and in small chunks of learning. His main barrier was writing. Harry was allocated a Chromebook and access to the Read and Write Toolbar. The toolbar had a variety of features to reduce the learning demand and cognitive load. The main accessibility feature Harry needed was the speech-to-text function. This enabled Harry to record all his ideas without the pressure of writing. Harry was able to produce longer pieces of writing in line with his peers, which he then printed off to edit. Using assistive technology removed a learning barrier and raised Harry's self-esteem.
5. **Social: Confidence.** Harry found navigating the busy, unstructured social times of the school day the most difficult. He found maintaining friendships difficult and playing collaboratively with peers. Through his time in the nurture class, he had the opportunity to rehearse social scenarios in a safe and supportive environment. He had daily access to structured games as well as the opportunity to reflect on games he could use again at lunchtime. Harry needed to make a plan with a trusted adult before heading out to play. He would identify who he was going to play with and what they were going to do. Harry was regularly encouraged to participate in the structured activities led by sports coaches at lunchtime or to attend a lunchtime

club where activities were structured. If there was an incident between himself and a peer, a consistent, restorative conversation would happen to ensure there was a resolution and a preventative plan for if a similar situation happened again. Harry built up a bank of social scenarios and scripts. These strategies, again, were added to his personalised toolkit to help him progress with his self-management skills.

Summary

Harry accessed Nurture for two terms before he was fully integrated back into his mainstream class. All of Harry's strategies were maintained to ensure he was successful at engaging in his learning. Harry had continued pastoral support to manage his anxiety by accessing a weekly Emotional Literacy Support Assistant (ELSA) session. An Education Health Care Plan was applied for and was successful in ensuring the level of support Harry needed was maintained.

The baseline assessments were repeated to get the exit data because he was finishing the nurture intervention.

Table 8.4 Final SDQ Outcomes (Exit Data)

	Teacher		*Parent*	
Combined Scores	*Score*	*Outcome*	*Score*	*Outcome*
Emotional Problems Scale	1	Close to Average	6	High
Conduct Problems Scale	3	Slightly Raised	3	Slightly Raised
Hyperactivity Scale	2	Close to Average	5	Close to Average
Peer Problems Scale	4	Slightly Raised	6	Very High
Pro-Social Scale	8	Close to Average	9	Close to Average
Externalising Score	5	Slightly Raised	8	Slightly Raised
Internalising Score	5	Slightly Raised	12	High
Total Difficulty Score	10	Close to Average	20	Very High
Impact Score	1	Slightly Raised	1	Slightly Raised

Reader Reflection

Have you collected a detailed pupil voice to understand the pupil's perspective?

How can you make your student feel safe and secure?

Do you have an assessment tool to measure entry and exit data?

Removal of barriers is key to pupil success and building self-esteem. Assistive technology can be a tool that can facilitate access to English and the wider curriculum.

Notes

1 Anderson A (2022) *Learning Through Play for Children with PMLD and Complex Needs: Using Purposeful Play to Support Cognition, Mental Health and Well-Being*. Abingdon: Routledge.
2 Rights of Every Child (1990) www.Unicef.org.uk 21st July 2024.
3 Alexander. R (2009) The Condition and Future of Primary Education. www.robinalexander.org.uk 17 May 2019.
4 McIntosh. J (2015) Final Report of The Commission on Assessment Without Levels. assets.publishing.service.gov.uk 17 May 2017
5 Rochford. D (2016) he Rochford Review: final report. Review of assessment for pupils working below the standard of national curriculum tests. www.gov.uk/government/publications/rochford-review-final-report 18th August 2024.
6 Sheridan. M. (1993) Spontaneous Play in Early Childhood, from Birth to Six Years. Routledge: London.
7 The Royal College of Speech and Language (2013) Inclusive Communication. www.rcslt.org/speech-and-language-therapy/inclusive-communication-overview 18th July 2024.
8 MacIntyre. C (2010) 2nd Edition Play for Children with Special Needs, Supporting Children with Learning Differences 3–9. Routledge: London and New York.
9 Carpenter. B, Egerton. J, Cockbill, Bloom. T, Fotheringham. J, Rawson. H, and Thistlewaite. J (2015). Engaging Learners with Complex Learning Difficulties and Disabilities. Routledge: London and New York.
10 SEN Code of Practice (2015).

INDEX

Note: Page numbers in *italics* indicate figures and in **bold** indicate tables on the corresponding pages.

For Product Safety Concerns and Information please contact our EU
representative GPSR@taylorandfrancis.com
Taylor & Francis Verlag GmbH, Kaufingerstraße 24, 80331 München, Germany

www.ingramcontent.com/pod-product-compliance
Lightning Source LLC
LaVergne TN
LVHW081151110826
845149LV00009B/1619